HOLIER

THAN

THOU

Ergun Mehmet Caner

HOLIER THAN THOU

When Faith Becomes Toxic

Abingdon Press
Nashville

HOLIER THAN THOU
WHEN FAITH BECOMES TOXIC

This book is printed on acid-free paper.

Library of Congress Cataloging-in-Publication Data

Caner, Ergun Mehmet.
   Holier than thou : when faith becomes toxic / Ergun Mehmet Caner.
      p. cm.
   ISBN 978-0-687-65840-4 (pbk. : alk. paper)
   1. Christian life. 2. Religious addiction—Christianity. 3. Compulsive behavior—Religious aspects—Christianity. 4. Pharisees—Miscellanea. I. Title.

   BV4501. 3. C3595 2009
   248—dc22

                                                                                2009008718

09 10 11 12 13 14 15 16 17 18—10 9 8 7 6 5 4 3 2
MANUFACTURED IN THE UNITED STATES OF AMERICA

Dedicated to Melvin Hilliard (1941–2007).
I doubt if I have ever met any man who demanded
more authenticity from Christians or Christianity than
Melvin. In his sixty-six years, Melvin had seen every
Christian scheme and scam known to man. Yet instead
of becoming cynical, he developed an incisive sense of
humor concerning life and faith. I do not think I ever
worked as hard to win one man's trust as I did to win
Melvin's. He was a transparent man,
and he made me one as well.

Acknowledgments

The majority of this book was written during the spring and summer of 2008, but the nexus for the book had been percolating for more than twenty years. A series of two articles in *Christian Counseling* on toxic faith garnered the interest of Dr. Kathy Armistead at Abingdon Press. I am grateful for her trust in me and her willingness to tolerate an intractable schedule by a harried author.

The book received its final edit during a weeklong intensive in Athens, Greece, at the Greek Bible Institute, on Marathon Road, in July 2008. I am grateful for the help and wisdom of Dr. John Gianopolis, along with the students, faculty, and staff of the Greek Bible Institute.

Finally, this book never would have seen the light of day were it not for the leadership and students of Liberty University. Our chancellor, Jerry Falwell Jr., has allowed me to continue leading the seminary in my most unorthodox manner. His trust in me and his leadership of our university have made my life a pure joy. The student body at Liberty University is the most committed band of believers I have ever had the pleasure of serving. The students demand absolute abandonment to the will of God. They have taught me far more than I could ever teach them.

Contents

Confessions of a Former Pharisee

It is difficult to pray when both of your legs are fast asleep. Trust me, I know.

As I knelt in the darkened dorm room, the sound of one of my roommates praying was only sporadically interrupted by the shuffling of legs and the faint groaning and creaking of sore knees and spines. This was more than just a prayer meeting; it was a marathon session. It was a competition.

Some hours before, one of my preacher buddies had enthusiastically suggested that we all join together in prayer to begin the new semester right. We were all young freshmen, and we were all preachers in training. We had known each other for precisely two weeks, and this was the first spiritual gathering we were to have at our own initiative. Ten of us gathered together at 7:00 p.m., and we circled up. Some of us sat, and others knelt. I was vaguely excited about the prospect of bombarding heaven with our earnest, if somewhat naive, prayers.

As the first young minister prayed, I adjusted my legs and listened intently. This was my first prayer session; I wanted to do it right. However, I had not accounted for the *prolonged* sessions of prayer. Each of the young preacher boys in that room was intent upon "outpraying" the next guy. As each person prayed on and on, I began to silently count who was up and how much time he took. By the time number six had finished, my legs were asleep. It was almost 9:00 p.m.

One young man seemed focused on mentioning every country he could remember. Another prayed for his extended family, which apparently numbered in the thousands. Another prayed for the missionaries he knew. I began to feel guilty for my discomfort and poor attitude. Surely, I thought, I was not as mature as these brothers, who could pray for hours.

Still, I could not ignore the pain I was experiencing. My knees ached against the hard tile floor. Sitting cross-legged only alleviated the pain briefly, until both feet were asleep again, and I had to readjust. At 9:30 p.m. it was my turn to pray. I felt bad for having checked my watch, and I said so at the outset of my prayer. I attempted to pray for my professors and classes, and my family. However, I became increasingly aware that I was praying publicly. Embarrassingly, my thought was, *I had better make this good.* My new friends were listening.

I don't know if you have ever been in such a circumstance, but I still feel sheepish about it, some twenty-five years later. I actually attempted to conjure up some "good words" that would impress Rick, Larry, Jeff, Steve, and the rest of them. And secretly, I had reduced prayer to a competition! I had to outpray them.

I was slowly becoming a modern Pharisee. It was the first time, but not the last, that I would be confronted with my own pseudospirituality. I was a legalist in the making. I was becoming toxic.

Catching Up on the Learning Curve

At that point in my life, I had been a Christian less than two years, and the grace of Jesus Christ was still fresh and new to me. I was raised in Islam, and when I became a Christian in 1982, I lost everything—my family, my friends, my mosque, my culture, even my identity. My father disowned me, but my church family adopted me.

It was a difficult transition at first. I had never held a Bible, a hymnal, or a Sunday school quarterly. I was unaccustomed to the language of the church. I did not even know what a bulletin was.

In addition, I was forced to adjust to life without my father. In many countries, including my home country of Turkey, to become a *murtad* (convert from Islam) was a capital crime, punishable by death within the span of twenty-four hours from indictment. Being disowned was a decidedly less horrific option, but no less traumatic to an eighteen-year-old young man.

A year following my conversion, I had surrendered to the gospel ministry. I did not know why I felt God wanted me in the ministry, but it was an undeniable and irresistible urge that consumed me. I stepped forward one Sunday morning in my church and made my intentions public. From that point on, I became one of the "preacher boys."

There were quite a number of us preachers in training at our small church in Columbus, Ohio. At regular intervals we preached on Sunday evenings. Oh, those poor church members! Even though they were subjected to some of the worst pulpit gems in recorded history, they still smiled, shook our hands, and found something kind to say. By the summer of 1984, I was a licensed minister, and my church held a reception to see me off as I traveled south to a small college in Kentucky, where I would begin training for the ministry.

Over the next five years, I became increasingly invested in the Christian culture. Virtually every person in my circle was studying for the ministry. We traveled on weekends to conduct youth revivals. We sang in the college choir. We had the same classes, the same professors, and many of the same aspirations. Yet we did not all *mature* at the same rate.

Some became stable and responsible ministers. Their walk and devotion to God were a constant and steady journey. Others became voices of change and revival. Their abundant faith and overflowing joy were contagious. Their churches grew and their ministries flourished.

My story was different. By the time I graduated from college, *I was . . . angry.*

I was uncertain exactly at whom I was angry. Perhaps myself. Perhaps God. Perhaps my perpetually happy friends. One certainty was that my condition was not their fault. It was mine. Yet I was incapable of resolving my problem. In the brief span of five years, I had gone from a joyous recipient of grace to a brooding, temperamental, judgmental man.

Pharisees like Me: Defining Some Terms

In virtually every church, there are one or two people just like I was. They can sap the life out of a worship service with one glance or word. They are judgmental to the point of being rude. It seems that they are happy only when others are as miserable as they are.

Throughout this book, we shall enlarge on some key principles that will guide us away from toxic faith. Perhaps they began as earnest, fervent believers; perhaps they have been betrayed and grown bitter. However they began their faith journey, somewhere they stepped off the path, and they are now looking for company. More people leave the church because of them than because of anything else. Often, they are only too willing to open the back door and usher people on their way out. They may not be bad people, but they do not (and perhaps can no longer) inspire Christian faith in others. Toxic Christians have sin-sick souls; their faith is viral, critical, delusional, and competitive.

1. Toxic Faith Is Viral

We can understand toxic Christians as pharisees or legalists. Like a virus, their bitterness spreads and infects wherever they go. They are legalistic to the point of paralysis. Once toxic Christians get a following in your church, their power knows no bounds! They spread quickly, using biblical terms to justify their beliefs. Please understand that I am using the term *pharisee* as an adjective to describe someone with unhealthy Christian faith and not as a put-down directed toward a person of Jewish faith or heritage.

2. Toxic Faith Is Critical

Every church has at least one person who believes that criticism is his or her spiritual gift. These persons offer weekly words of discouragement in the service. They rise in every business meeting, not with solutions but with censure. Rarely do toxic persons accomplish anything, but as one older preacher said, they have "denunciation in their wings." They are defined by what they are against rather than what they are for.

3. Toxic Faith Is Delusional

One of the most frustrating dimensions of their disease is that they *believe* that they are actually fine! The rest of the world is messed up, in their way of thinking. In fact, they would put up their holiness against that of anyone in the church. Even this soon in our analysis, you have probably thought of someone who fits in this category. The bad news is, if that person were to pick up this book, read it, outline it, and highlight it, he or she still would not see himself or herself in its pages.

True, complete pharisees are deluded into thinking that their standards are quite comfortable. When questioned about the biblical basis for their beliefs, pharisees always answer with tradition. They have sustained this high level for a long period of their lives, and have justified their actions for so long, they wonder why you do not see the "logic" of their beliefs.

4. Toxic Faith Is Competitive

For poisonous pharisees, Christianity is a competition. It is not enough to be good Christians; they must be better than *you*. They often measure holiness by comparing themselves to other people.

When a topic as incendiary as this is addressed, it is probably best to explain some terms. *Legalism* is a movement within Christianity that defines holiness by self-made standards. There are certain issues in everyday life that are explicit in the Bible. Issues such as prayer, sexual purity, biblical fidelity, and the importance of the local church are not only explicit in the Bible, but they are in the black-and-white category. They are not up for a debate. They can be categorized as absolutes.

Other tangents off those absolutes are not so clear. Legalism thrives on taking those murky areas and superimposing absolute standards on them. For example, I remember one Sunday in my church the pastor moved the offering from right before the message to right at the end of the service. You would have thought that he slapped the pianist! The uproar was quite substantial. One member in the parking lot remarked, "If he does that again, I am leaving the church! That just isn't biblical!"

Now, does the Bible stipulate exactly when the offering should be taken in the worship service? No, it does not. But in legalism, the methods we use become as sacred as the principle behind those methods. Taking up the offering is a biblical principle. When you take up the offering can be placed in the category of preference. A principle is a firm and clear issue, doctrine, or ethic in the Bible.

For the legalist, preference is the same as principle. A *preference*, however, is simply the way you *like something done*. It is the method you choose to use. This distinction is lost on legalists because the lines are blurred. To them, *preference is principle.*

Many readers may begin this book and become uncomfortable, as some of the descriptions and narratives may come painfully close to their own reality. It is certainly not my intention to make you, the reader, uncomfortable. Neither is it my purpose to make you feel as if I am purposefully taking shots at people in a type of literary revenge. That is not my intent at all.

This is a work of admission of my own failings, weaknesses, and vulnerabilities. Consider this a modern mea culpa, in the vein of such works as Augustine's *Confessions.* Likewise, there are degrees of toxicity, but be assured that the end result is as bad—or worse—than I describe.

Life and Times of Jesus

I do not believe any Christian sets out to become a pharisee; it just develops over time. Much like one experiences the aging process, one becomes accustomed to subtle changes in behavior. It is not until one looks back in retrospect that these changes become evident. I also believe this was the case in Jesus' time.

Throughout the Gospels, the religious leaders of the synagogues in Israel hounded Jesus. They were more than just the *pastors*, to use our modern terminology. They were judge and jury for any sin that was committed in the Holy Land. While the Roman government regulated the citizenship laws, the Jewish leaders controlled all violations of religious ordinances.

This made a difficult and tense relationship between the synagogue and the Roman state. When Jesus was being tried after his arrest, his captors led him from one courthouse to the next, as the charges against him were both civil (treason) and religious (blasphemy). In Matthew 27:1-2, we read: "Early in the morning, all the chief priests and the elders of the people came to the decision to put Jesus to death. They bound him, led him away and handed him over to Pilate, the governor."

Since the Jewish leaders wanted Jesus put to death, they tried to get Pilate, the governor, to execute him for the crime of treason.

Pilate did not feel that Jesus was guilty of the crime against the state, however. The vivid narrative in Matthew 27:22-25 reads like a drama as the crowd in the public square made their voices heard:

> "What shall I do, then, with Jesus who is called Christ?" Pilate asked. They all answered, "Crucify him!" "Why? What crime has he committed?" asked Pilate. But they shouted all the louder, "Crucify him!" When Pilate saw that he was getting nowhere, but that instead an uproar was starting, he took water and washed his hands in front of the crowd. "I am innocent of this man's blood," he said. "It is your responsibility!" All the people answered, "Let his blood be on us and on our children!"

Pharisees: The Legalists of the Lord's Day

Throughout this book, we shall be determining the symptoms of this poison. The term *pharisees* has been tossed around so freely that it has largely lost any meaning. Although often stereotyped, Pharisees were, like any group of people, a varied lot. And some Pharisees were converted to the Christian faith, most notably Paul. But in the Gospel of Matthew, we follow them as they hound Jesus. They were some of the religious leaders of their day, just as some toxic Christians are leaders in our churches today. Sometimes it is too easy to point fingers and place oneself in the judgment seat. Only God can judge, but through God's grace, Jesus calls all of us to repentance, even those of us with pharisaical tendencies.

The Pharisees appear quite often in the Gospels, ninety-four times to be exact. Although each of the other Jewish political parties—the Essenes, Zealots, and Sadducees—had conservative and legalistic tendencies, the Pharisees are especially singled out.

Josephus noted there were as many as six thousand Pharisees in Jesus' time.They did not believe that the Torah was the only source of truth for the Jews. They recognized the oral traditions as equal to the Old Testament. These oral traditions were stories passed down from rulings and teachings by wise men who commented on the written word. These commentaries eventually became a collection known as the Talmud.

The Pharisees despised the Roman rulers who reigned over Jerusalem. They were theocrats who wanted to establish a common law based on Leviticus. Doctrinally, they believed in good and evil angels who waged a war in the heavens over the souls of humanity. In many ways, they were a very mystical branch of Judaism.

Above all, the Pharisees believed in outward piety. More than anything, the Pharisees wanted the respect and admiration of others, especially concerning their personal and public devotion. In public they prayed loudly and strictly followed the Law. They went through intricate public washings in the baptismal font, known as the *miqvah*. They made a big show of their fasting and gave their alms in a very public manner. Jesus often rebuked them for their hollow public deeds because they were for show only. A Pharisee was generally more concerned with outward appearance than inner devotion.

Even Jesus' forerunner, John the Baptist, held the Pharisees in contempt for their political maneuvering. Right before he baptized Jesus at the beginning of Jesus' ministry, John saw a group of religious leaders gathering on the banks of the Jordan River. When he spoke, John did not welcome them as honored guests! Read what happened: "When he saw many of the Pharisees and Sadducees coming to where he was baptizing, he said to them: 'You brood of vipers! Who warned you to flee from the coming wrath?'" (Matthew 3:7). It is doubtful that referring to the Pharisees as a "brood of vipers" would have earned John an invitation to speak at their annual convention.

Sadducees: The Rationalists of the Lord's Day

A major opposing party to the Pharisees in Jewish politics and philosophy was known as the Sadducees. Mentioned fourteen times in the New Testament, the Sadducees opposed virtually every doctrine held by the Pharisees. The Sadducees denied the resurrection of the body, the immortality of the soul, and the existence of angels or even spirits. Luke 20:27 notes, "Some of the Sadducees, who say there is no resurrection, came to Jesus with a question."

They were the intelligentsia, the philosophers and rational thinkers. They denied any oral tradition or teachings and held to the written Torah (the first five books of the Bible) alone as the authority for life and practice. The Apostle Paul used the political fighting between the Pharisees and the Sadducees to his advantage during his final days. When Paul was facing threats, imprisonment, and death from the religious rulers, he sparked a fight between them on purpose. Acts 23:6-8 records,

> Then Paul, knowing that some of them were Sadducees and the others Pharisees, called out in the Sanhedrin, "My brothers, I am a Pharisee, the son of a Pharisee. I stand on trial because of my hope in the resurrection of the dead." When he said this, a dispute broke out between the Pharisees and the Sadducees, and the assembly was divided. (The Sadducees say that there is no resurrection, and that there are neither angels nor spirits, but the Pharisees acknowledge them all.)

Ironically, the Pharisees and the Sadducees came together for one common purpose—the attempt to silence Jesus of Nazareth. Matthew 16:1 tells us of this uncomfortable alliance: "The Pharisees and Sadducees came to Jesus and tested him by asking him to show them a sign from heaven."

Sanhedrin: The Supreme Court of the Lord's Day

The highest judicial council of Jesus' day was known as the Sanhedrin. The name comes from the Greek term *synedrion*, which means "sitting together." It roughly translates into "council" or "assembly." Tradition teaches that the Sanhedrin consisted of seventy or seventy-one members, who ruled on Jewish religious matters. In other words, they were a type of religious senate.

The reason for the Sanhedrin was simple. Once Judea, Samaria, and the surrounding area fell into the hands of the Roman Empire, the legal codes changed. As the Roman Empire expanded, it encompassed lands with strong religious communities like the Jewish people. Rather than force their rule completely on these peoples, they allowed them to establish their own religious courts, which would be the final word in matters of religious law. Rome felt it would placate these distant lands and make them feel as if they had a voice in their existence.

The threat posed by Jesus' radical teachings did not raise up scattered and unorganized opposition. In fact, the entire Sanhedrin committed to stopping him. The Bible records, "The chief priests and the whole Sanhedrin were looking for false evidence against

Jesus so that they could put him to death" (Matthew 26:59). The highest and most influential religious group of his time was committed to Jesus' demise.

But even within the Sanhedrin, it is likely that Jesus had sympathizers or perhaps followers. Consider Nicodemus. According to John 3:1, Nicodemus was a leader of the Jews. Modern scholars think this meant that he was a member of the Sanhedrin. Also consider Joseph of Arimathea, who was a Jewish leader (see Mark 15:42-46 and Luke 23:50-54) and was called a disciple of Jesus (John 19:38). So while the Jewish leaders were not of one mind concerning Jesus, there were sufficient numbers who wanted him permanently silenced.

Scribes: The Theologians of the Lord's Day

The scribes were like our modern seminary professors. Mark 7:5 refers to them as the "teachers of the law." Having studied intensely in an apprenticeship, a scribe would become a walking encyclopedia of Judaic knowledge. In many ways scribes served as religious judges, offering opinions on such issues as the methods for washing hands before a meal.

When Jesus finally responded to the perpetual accusations thrown at him, he reserved some of his strongest language for the scribes: "The teachers of the law and the Pharisees sit in Moses' seat. . . . Woe to you, teachers of the law and Pharisees, you hypocrites! You shut the kingdom of heaven in men's faces. You yourselves do not enter, nor will you let those enter who are trying to" (Matthew 23:2, 13). The scribes were the final word in these rulings. As those who sat in "Moses' seat," they often viewed their own rulings as equal to those of Scripture.

The Pathology of Crazies: How Did We Get like This?

How did religious people end up uniting against the Lord of heaven when he was on the earth? How did they come to the point of uniting in hatred against one man? I believe it was pathological, and I will leave you with one final illustration to explain the process.

By way of confession, I am germaphobic. I know there is a technical term for it, but germaphobic is far easier to understand.

No kidding. No exaggeration.

This makes life tough as a minister, especially when *shaking hands* is required.

I admit it. After a Sunday service—when I shake the hands of parishioners for an extended period of time—I scrub my hands like a heart surgeon. I do not mean to be offensive, but have you ever watched people in church before they shake your hand?

I often see them out of the corner of my eye. I attempt to maintain a conversation with the person in front of me, but instead I see *them* scratching, shifting, and readjusting. In general terms, they are grooming . . . with their hands.

Immediately after the service, all I can think is, *How can I get to a restroom? Does anyone have hand sanitizer? Was that man infected?* I scrub under my nails. I thoroughly scour my hands, up to my wrists. On occasion, I even run into other church members doing the same thing. We look at one another sheepishly, as if we share a common addiction.

Now, let me ask you, does this make me insane? Does this qualify me as obsessive-compulsive? Am I certifiable?

Perhaps I am just idiosyncratic. Perhaps I am merely clean. In any case, it does not make me *pathological*, and that is the operative difference.

Being pathological is destructive. In the context of Christianity, pathological people are people who are not merely carriers; they are infectious. Pathological Christians are toxic. They destroy relationships and leave a trail of human wreckage. Being idiosyncratic is usually just amusing to other people. On occasion, fellow Christians will pull me aside and exclaim that they share the same germaphobia. They surreptitiously show me a gallon jug of antibacterial lotion in their purses. But I do not have to touch a doorknob fifteen times before I open a door.

Toxic faith and pathological Christianity are an entirely different breed. It is a poisonous strain of "faith" that tears down much more quickly than it ever lifts up. It is a virus. It is not merely a personal affliction; it spreads. It contaminates and pollutes; and if left unchecked, it can taint an entire fellowship of believers.

It is a poisonous strain of pseudopiety, and it has a name. For our purposes, we shall call it the "poison of the pharisees."

Salvation Is Eternal; Crazy Is Forever

Anyone can become susceptible to the pharisees' poison because it is an insidious disease. Good and godly people can become pharisaical if they do not recognize the subtle symptoms. It is usually a disease that the carrier never recognizes. Others will see it in you before you see it in yourself.

Some cases are benign. Some people may be normal 95 percent of the time, but then suddenly, they become raging and angry Christians who lash out at everyone else's failings. In an instant, they become poisonous. Though they can be toxic, they are usually harmless. In a short period of time, they recover and usually apologize profusely to everyone they attacked. They do not carry grudges or instigate further assaults.

Some Christians are terminal. They have been pharisaical for such an extended period that they no longer recognize the symptoms. They desire no cure. They have grown accustomed to being toxic, and perhaps they even like it. Let me further explain.

Usually in every church, there is at least one person who is certifiable. This person changes the very nature of the room by entering it. When he raises his hand during a prayer meeting, all others in attendance collectively hold their breath. He is never happy and seems to almost gain pleasure from his misery. When you run into him, you kick yourself for asking him how he is because you know he will tell you!

When you see pharisees coming down the hallway, you usually duck into a side room because you know you will have an encounter with them and the storm cloud they rode in on. This is not to doubt their salvation. They probably are saved. They are just not very happy about it. They barely tolerate Jesus, much less his followers! One wise sage noted, "Salvation is eternal, but crazy is forever."

Neither is this an indictment of you, the reader. You have tried, really tried. You have talked to them, prayed with them, and counseled them. You have stayed on the phone listening to them complain about the minute details of perceived offense they have suffered. Yet nothing has worked. In fact, the more you counsel them, the worse they get! Often when you leave their presence, you feel depressed and despondent. You have been infected, and you were on a mission of mercy.

You do not wish them ill; but you wish, deeply in your heart, that they would choose to embrace the blessings of God rather than the curses they see. You feel a sense of futility when they approach because it is akin to beating your head against a wall. No matter what you say, they will not be satisfied. You feel drained and tired after being with them, even for only a short time. You wonder, *Why do they come to me?* Secretly, you know that they have annoyed most others in the church to the point of distraction. Your heart is pure, but your flesh is weary. You want them in heaven, but you just pray that they are not living beside you!

You have unwittingly been exposed to the toxin of the pharisees.

This book has been written to detoxify your soul and bring back the joy of your salvation. Enjoy the journey . . . and do not forget to wash your hands.

CHAPTER ONE

For There to Be Winners,
There Also Have to Be Losers

*Do not think that I have come to abolish the Law or the
Prophets; I have not come to abolish them but to fulfill them. I
tell you the truth, until heaven and earth disappear, not the
smallest letter, not the least stroke of a pen, will by any means
disappear from the Law until everything is accomplished.
Anyone who breaks one of the least of these commandments and
teaches others to do the same will be called least in the kingdom
of heaven, but whoever practices and teaches these commands
will be called great in the kingdom of heaven. For I tell you that
unless your righteousness surpasses that of the Pharisees and the
teachers of the law, you will certainly not enter the kingdom of
heaven. (Matthew 5:17-20)*

Guess Who Grandma Loves the Most?

When we were young, my brothers and I had a game we loved
to play.

It was called "Guess who Grandma loves the most?"

The game usually began when we were drawing pictures. All
three boys took great care in drawing some random picture. We
were typical boys, so we drew a lot of cars, planes, and motor-
cycles. The secret was, we never signed our names to our pictures.
We laid them out on the table and summoned our grandmother.
We called her "Mormor," which means "mother's mother."

"Mormor," we asked eagerly, "which picture do you like the
best?"

Our grandmother was much too wise to fall for such a trick, and she smiled and said, "I love all of them the same."

"No!" we insisted. "Which one do you love more than the other two?"

"I love all three drawings," she stated firmly, "and I love all three of my grandsons."

In our little world, this competition was incessant, repetitive, and essential. We just knew that if she would give an honest answer, we would discover who was the favorite. Since we were equally pathetic artists, we hoped that she would pick the picture based purely on maternal grounds.

What made this rivalry even more poignant was that, in my heart of hearts, I *knew* that my grandmother loved my youngest brother, Emir, more. I was the oldest of the three brothers, which meant I was saddled with the brunt of the chores in the house. Erdem, the next in line, was always a meticulous boy. He kept his side of the room spotless and organized to the point of distraction. In retrospect, I think it was a disease of some sort. After all, how many ten-year-old boys keep their books and videos in alphabetical order on the shelves and indexed in a binder?

I was more of a free spirit. In our home, my eccentric ways were legendary. I thumb-tacked my clean clothes on the wall. Thus, I instantly knew which clothes were clean and which were dirty. My side of the room usually looked like an archaeological dig. Contrasted with my slovenly ways, the ways of Erdem the Obsessive-Compulsive earned major points.

Compared to Emir, however, Erdem and I might as well have been two homeless squatters living on the lawn. Since Emir was born last, Mormor played a larger part in raising him. Both of our parents were working; and as Erdem and I went off to school, Mormor and Emir spent countless hours together. They developed a bond that was unbreakable. I have often stated that if Emir and I were in a car wreck, I could be covered in blood and have bones protruding from my flesh, and Mormor would step over me to get to Emir, who would be unscathed.

When called upon to do chores, all Emir had to do was muster a feeble cough, and he was relieved of duty. By simply rubbing his head and moaning slightly, Emir could get out of anything. The workload fell onto my shoulders. As I shuffled out the door, I angrily saw Emir, standing behind Mormor, with a slight smile, waving and pointing. I wanted to stab him in the neck—such brotherly love.

This ongoing rivalry fed the comparison beast. We spent hours plotting against one another, attempting to earn her favor. The key point was, it was not enough for Mormor to love us unconditionally. She had to love us *more* than the others.

Toxic Christianity approaches God in precisely the same way. It is not enough that Christ loves us totally and completely. For the pharisee to be happy, God must love him or her *more* than God loves you. This form of competitive Christianity is a performance-based system, and it is soul-numbingly wearisome. It can drain you of your joy and rob you of your freedom in Christ. Christianity becomes a horrible reality show where you must scheme to get everyone else thrown off the island.

Jesus saw this coming right from the start.

The Hopes of Happiness: The Sermon on the Mount

The crowd gathered anxiously to see Jesus. The rumor was that Jesus had disappeared into the desert for more than a month. One man postulated that he had heard that Jesus was fighting the devil himself! In any regard, his long absence was over, and the people rejoiced to see him back in his environs.

Even today, the acoustics are amazing on the side of those steep hills around the Sea of Galilee. It was like being in a well-designed amphitheater, and all in attendance could hear the words of this prophet about whom they had heard so much. The crowd pressed in to see this gaunt man with the darkened skin. He was seated on the ground, on the upper part of the slope. His disciples sat in a semicircle around him. The starvation during his temptations took quite a toll on his body, and the forty-day sun deepened the color of his already olive skin.

Makairos, he began (in the Greek), "happy."

It seemed an odd choice for someone who obviously suffered a recent traumatic experience. Why would he begin with the word *happy*?

Nine times he repeated the word: *makairos*. Happy. Blessed. Content. Fulfilled.

Nine times he offered the conditions of this abiding peace he was offering:

> Blessed are the poor in spirit,
>   for theirs is the kingdom of heaven.
> Blessed are those who mourn,
>   for they will be comforted.
> Blessed are the meek,
>   for they will inherit the earth.
> Blessed are those who hunger and thirst for righteousness,
>   for they will be filled.
> Blessed are the merciful,
>   for they will be shown mercy.
> Blessed are the pure in heart,
>   for they will see God.
> Blessed are the peacemakers,
>   for they will be called sons of God.
> Blessed are those who are persecuted because of
>   righteousness,
>   for theirs is the kingdom of heaven.
> Blessed are you when people insult you, persecute you and falsely say all kinds of evil against you because of me. Rejoice and be glad, because great is your reward in heaven, for in the same way they persecuted the prophets who were before you. (Matthew 5:3-12)

Each "Blessed" seemed to invert common logic and thinking. The poor should be happy because the kingdom of heaven is theirs? When does that take place? The meek will overthrow brutal dictators? I am blessed when people insult me? I don't feel blessed. Jesus was certainly offering a new approach.

He continued speaking, comparing the believers to salt and light. They were compelled to actually come in contact with a desperate world, like salt applied as a preservative to meat. They were to let their light shine before all people, without fear of consequence (Matthew 5:13-16).

However, his tone changed when he introduced a new topic: the Law of God. His words are recorded in Matthew 5:17 and the following verses. For any devout Jew, Jesus was about to unleash his message with clarity.

What the Law Cannot Do (Matthew 5:17-37)

Jesus began by stating that his mission was to completely fulfill all the obligations of the Law. This sacred word came from God, in burning bushes not consumed, from mountaintops in the desert. Carried along with the vestments and precious materials this Law demanded, the Law symbolized their intimate connection to God. However, the Law—complete with festivals and feasts listed therein—actualized the covering of their sin. With wave offerings, grain offerings, doves, and sheep carried up the temple steps, the Law was a how-to guide for forgiveness from guilt and eternal death.

Perhaps the people believed that Jesus was coming to destroy the forms and functions of Judaism. Perhaps they wondered if he was bringing them a new way to God. Or perhaps Jesus just understood the fear in the hearts of his listeners. In the "Blessed" sermon, he had just told them that persecution was inevitable, and then in his salt-and-light teaching, he told them to confront this hostile world. He said that the Law would completely fulfill its purpose. The Law had a sacred purpose that would run its course.

Yet beginning in Matthew 5:19, Jesus began to logically place these laws in their context. If the Law is the measuring stick of righteousness, then will heaven be closest for those who followed most closely? Who among us, they must have wondered, is even close in following these edicts that are so numerous and specific? Jewish scholars such as Rambam have counted 613 major commandments. They delineate acts while asleep, when getting out of bed, methods of eating, commerce, and business, and every other arena of life. Does anyone have hope if the stick is 613 units high? I might as well give up now, since I believe I have broken four of them while typing this last sentence!

That was Jesus' point exactly. In Matthew 5:19, he stated that if you break the smallest and seemingly least consequential law, you will stand guilty before God and barely make it into heaven. No, Jesus continued, the only people who make it in will be those who completely follow the Law to the letter. Only those who follow perfectly will be called perfect.

Depressing, isn't it? I can go all day and not swear, or even yell at an innocent person; but if I swallow an accidental nut on Yom

5

Kippur, I can end up a maid in someone else's mansion in Glory. Or perhaps there will be no eternal life for me at all.

Great Analogy; Bad Timing

Jesus' final sentence is most evocative, however. He stated, "For I tell you that unless your righteousness surpasses that of the Pharisees and the teachers of the law, you will certainly not enter the kingdom of heaven" (Matthew 5:20). Reread that sentence. Did Jesus mean that even the highest, most prominent religious rulers of their time would *not* be going to heaven?

That is exactly what he meant.

His precise wording left little to question. For the common man and woman to make it into heaven, they would have to go farther than the Pharisees and scribes. The Pharisees and scribes did not go far enough.

To further cement his position, Jesus cited specific examples of the Pharisees' mindless obedience. He used a great phrase to tie down his points again and again: "You have heard that it was said. . . . But I tell you. . . ." The chart on the following page might help:

You Have Heard That It Was Said	But I Tell You
"Do not murder, and anyone who murders will be subject to judgment." (5:21)	Anyone who is angry with his brother will be subject to judgment. (5:22)
Anyone who says to his brother, "Raca," is answerable to the Sanhedrin. (5:22)	But anyone who says, "You fool!" will be in danger of the fire of hell. (5:22)
"Do not commit adultery." (5:27)	Anyone who looks at a woman lustfully has already committed adultery with her in his heart. (5:28)
"Do not break your oath, but keep the oaths you have made to the Lord." (5:33)	Do not swear at all: either by heaven, for it is God's throne; or by the earth, for it is his footstool; or by Jerusalem, for it is the city of the Great King. And do not swear by your head, for you cannot make even one hair white or black. Simply let your "Yes" be "Yes," and your "No," "No"; anything beyond this comes from the evil one. (5:34-37)

At every juncture, Jesus peeled back the façade of mechanical actions that many Jews had followed in their sleep and revealed a deeper purpose or understanding of those laws.

Toxic Misunderstanding: The Practice of the Law

Jesus' reinterpretation of Jewish law profoundly overturned centuries of schizophrenia. The Jewish leaders acted as they wished in private, but put on great airs when they were being observed. They acted one way at home and yet another way in the synagogue.

Does this sound like anyone you may know?

The Pharisees were the emblem of hypocrisy. They compartmentalized their spiritual life and their political life. They could happily act one way with friends, as long as they returned to their solemnity while at the synagogue. Twice Jesus reminded them that he would rather have obedience, which is an act of the heart, than sacrifice, which can be done without any thought at all.

From the very beginning, Christianity was designed to begin inside out. Once the heart is softened to God, then the acts will follow. But having the acts without the heart is like wearing a wedding ring only when it fits *your* purposes. The Pharisees wanted the pomp and circumstance of the religious life, but they misunderstood the devotion to the God who gave them those rules.

Toxic Misunderstanding: The Purpose of the Law

By using the strict Law against even the Pharisees, our Lord illustrated another problem with lockstep legalism. The Jews in Jesus' time believed that by following the laws, they were making themselves "good enough" for heaven. There is only one problem. What is the central key to understanding the nature of the Law? The Law was never designed by God to make anyone good. The Law can only restrain evil.

> *The Law was never designed by God to make anyone good. The Law can only restrain evil.*

The Apostle Paul built on Jesus' premise in Galatians, when he called the Law a "tutor" that points us to the grace of God through Jesus Christ. Listen to Paul's vivid language: "Before faith came, we were kept in custody under the law, being shut up to the faith which was later to be revealed. Therefore the Law has become our tutor to lead us to Christ, so that we may be justified by faith" (Galatians 3:23-24 NASB).

Simple logic argues against anyone trying to make it into heaven by his or her own works. Here is a question that you can use to open a lively discussion in church, home, or school: If even one person could make it into heaven by following the Law, then does that not make Jesus' sacrifice on the cross and the resurrection unnecessary? If even one person, born with a sinful nature, is able to live an entire life without breaking any of the 613 laws in the Torah and Talmud, then Jesus wasted his time, and the rest of us are just lazy. That is why Paul also said, "If you receive circumcision, Christ will be of no benefit to you" (Galatians 5:2 NASB). It is either Christ's shed blood or the Law.

Gold Medals at the Pharisee Olympics

Thus, by listening to Jesus' words here in the text, we stumble upon the first fundamental principle of fakes, frauds, and pharisees. They live by a slogan: I don't have to be superholy to make it. All I have to do is to be holier than *you*.

Now you can understand why pharisees are always jumping on your case (which is translated into "rebuking you" in *Christianese*, the language of churches).

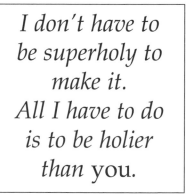

I don't have to be superholy to make it. All I have to do is to be holier than you.

They have to be constantly on the lookout for crimes and sins that they themselves do not commit. Then they must raise the decibel level tenfold in expressing their outrage. By pointing out your failure to everyone they know, they go up two steps at the pharisee Olympics, while you take a step backward.

The added bonus for this method of legalistic ballet is that it demands nothing of them! They now look holier just by standing next to you. It costs them nothing. But the final dividend for them is even more tragic. Each night, when they drift off to sleep, they can be comforted by the "fact" that now, since you are out of contention, they stand closer to God. And they can believe that God, indeed, loves them more.

CHAPTER TWO

The Holy Huddle

As Jesus went on from there, he saw a man named Matthew sitting at the tax collector's booth. "Follow me," he told him, and Matthew got up and followed him. While Jesus was having dinner at Matthew's house, many tax collectors and "sinners" came and ate with him and his disciples. When the Pharisees saw this, they asked his disciples, "Why does your teacher eat with tax collectors and 'sinners'?" On hearing this, Jesus said, "It is not the healthy who need a doctor, but the sick. But go and learn what this means: 'I desire mercy, not sacrifice.' For I have not come to call the righteous, but sinners." (Matthew 9:9-13)

Who Let the Dogs In?

When I was a college student, a church in the hills of southeastern Kentucky called me to be its youth pastor. There were only six young people in my first meeting, and none of them was particularly excited to have me as the new youth pastor. However, over the course of a few months, we grew to work together and became a team. There was no definable leader among the six, but one young man seemed the most open to me. He was just entering high school and had been raised in the church, so he had seen youth ministers come and go. He assumed that I was going to stay for a brief period of time and then leave as all the others had done.

But I not only fell in love with the people; I moved there. Instead of living in my college dorm and commuting on weekends, I moved to Manchester and settled into their community. It took time, but soon the young man understood that I was determined to become one of them. We would go to his house and swim in his family pool. We would drive around each Friday night, which was a high school ritual in Manchester. The route was through the town, from the Wal-Mart to the local grocery store, and it seemed hundreds of kids in cars followed it religiously. Though I was a twenty-one-year-old youth pastor, I did not let my outsider status dissuade me. Every Friday night, there I was in my old jalopy. The students gradually came to see that I was not the enemy.

The end result was that the youth group began to grow. Manchester was not a big town, but within a couple of years, we were averaging more than sixty youth each Sunday morning. The youth were bringing their friends, and their friends were becoming Christians.

The only problem was that most of these kids were not raised in the church and knew little of church protocols. They were Appalachian mountain kids and tough as a tenpenny nail. Some of them did not dress as fashionably as others because, quite frankly, they did not have the money. Many of the boys did not have Christian parents, so on Saturday nights, I picked them up at their homes and piled them in my car, and they spent the night sprawled all over the house. The next morning, I had a built-in team of workers who helped me set up chairs and set out Bibles.

What the boys lacked in decorum, they made up for in faith. In three years we went on three mission trips. These kids held Bible club meetings in backyards, went door to door witnessing, started a youth choir and drama team, and hosted countless youth revivals. They shared their faith freely, and Manchester buzzed with excitement. These students were claiming their schools for Christ, and as each young person became a Christian, he or she stood side by side with the friend who had invited him or her to church.

On one particular Sunday night, our youth did all the ministry while I preached. They said the prayers, took up the offering, led the worship, and formed the choir. Two girls even sang the special, which was a huge step for them. It was quite an experience to see them at work. After the service, they were greeted by grateful parents and proud grandparents who had wiped away tears as they watched this amazing group of kids proclaim Jesus.

Not everyone was happy, however. One older gentleman (let's call him Perry) pulled me aside during the reception in the fellowship hall. By the scowl on his face, I could tell that he was displeased with something. I was not on my guard, though, because he was one of those people who were *always* displeased. When he spoke, it was quite clear that this was not his normal gloomy disposition.

"Preacher," he began, "these kids just don't *fit* here." He emphasized the word *fit* with a particularly harsh tone. It was as if he was spitting the word rather than saying it. He continued, "I know half of these kids' fathers, and trust me, just as soon as you turn your back, they are going to steal something or cause some trouble. It's best if we don't let them in where they can do any damage to the church. I have known kids like this my entire life, son. They will *never* change."

There have been few times in my life when I have been left speechless, but that was one of them. I stood before him, shocked. I could not believe that someone was actually saying those words, especially in light of the service we had just experienced. Sensing my discomfort, he continued speaking, asking me if the church had approved of the young boys spending the night in the youth pastor's parsonage. I told him that I had received the parents' permission and that the senior pastor knew this was the only means of getting the boys to church on Sunday.

He concluded, "But, son, don't you know that if a minister from our church is *seen* with some of these kids, it will reflect poorly on the church? It just doesn't look right." With those final words, he immediately left me to complain directly to the pastor.

Symptoms of the Holy Huddle

We all know people like the aforementioned gentleman, don't we? They are the self-appointed watchdogs of the church. Never happy and perpetually offended, they patrol the church hallways, seeking offenses to their sensibilities. For people such as Perry, the church is only as effective as it is separate—and safe—from the world. I refer to these types of Christians as the Holy Huddle because they seem to view church as the one place in their lives where they are not infected by the downtrodden, the sinful, and the unfortunate. For them, church is a safe haven, from which they can hide from the world. They become indignant when people who are less schooled in the protocols of the church begin walking its halls.

When it comes to church, the Holy Huddle people seem to sing a classic song:

Us four . . .
No more . . .
And lock the door.

The symptoms of a Holy Huddle infection are quite subtle but also quite easy to spot. Trust me, if your church has these people in your fellowship, you will know it soon enough! They always make themselves known. They even did it in Jesus' time. We can see it in our text.

Notice the response from the Pharisees when they saw Jesus eating with the politicians and the sinners. They asked, "Why does your teacher eat with tax collectors and 'sinners'?" (Matthew 9:11). The Pharisees considered both groups the untouchables. For a believer to fellowship with these types of people was unthinkable to them.

Tax collectors were regarded as traitors in their time. Often they were Jews or countrymen who were hired by the Roman government to collect the taxes due to the emperor. They were usually harsh men, guilty of either taking bribes or pocketing some of the money. Like men who collected for loan sharks, they often used dubious methods to amass their quota. Why would Jesus even be seen with such vultures?

The second indictment was against the "sinners," which meant those who were publicly *known* as sinners. They were the people counted among the lowest strata of the cultural index. They usually lived in the equivalent of the red-light district of town and earned money by nefarious means. In modern terms, these were the prostitutes, the alcoholics, the topless dancers, the addicted, and the homeless. Why would Jesus be seen with them? Why would anyone?

When people are infected with the Holy Huddle disease, they become obsessed with appearances. They often cite the text, "Abstain from all appearance of evil" (1 Thessalonians 5:22 KJV), which to them means even coming in contact with those who practice evil. In their minds, being seen with a sinful person makes believers unclean.

In our modern Christian culture, this even extends to friendships. In certain denominations, churches practice secondary separation. This doctrine states that if you are friends with an unbeliever who is in public sin, I cannot be friends with you, because by your patronage, you too have become infected with the sin. They conclude that their reputation will be harmed as well if they are in fellowship with you.

In my final pastorate, I encountered such a charge. In Denver, Colorado, our little church was an oasis of faith, surrounded by many broken people. The streets surrounding the church were lined with cheap and dirty hotels, and homeless people often slept in the park across the street. In my mind, it was a perfect location for a church! That was not the consensus, however.

As the church began to grow, many of these people were coming to Christ. Virtually every week, people from all walks of life were becoming Christians in our church. Some of the young couples caught this vision, and soon our men's ministry began feeding homeless people on Saturdays and inviting them to church. The church began to be known as a haven for the hurting.

Many established leaders in our church were uncomfortable with the people who were coming to the services. One particular man asked to meet me in my office. He sat down and proceeded to tell me that he did not intend to have his daughters raised in a church with "these types" of people attending.

He was not mad, self-righteous, or mean in any fashion. He did not come across as arrogant or demeaning. He was firm and resolute. He did *not* want to go to church with these people. His reasoning sounded familiar. These new Christians, he stated, were not mature Christians. They were often loud and boisterous. They did not know how to act in church. They did not dress in clothes that reflected a Christian home. They were, in his estimation, a bad influence on the church and his family.

That day, he left our church and transferred to another one of his liking. He had been a leader and a rock in the church for years. He and his wife led countless ministries there, and now they were gone. I was crestfallen, but I was not surprised. It was the same reasoning that I had heard from Perry in Kentucky, some fifteen years before.

Jesus and the Untouchables:
The Woman at the Well (John 4:7-42)

Jesus' dinner with the politicans and sinners was not the only time Jesus encountered a charge of guilt by association. Perhaps there is no greater example of Jesus' flouting convention and religion than his encounter with the Samaritan woman (John 4). In this one meeting, Jesus violated a myriad of legalistic rules. For an iconoclast like myself, it is a juicy bit of adventure.

According to the religious games of his day, Jesus never should have spoken to the woman he met at the well. No self-respecting man, let alone a religious leader or a legalist, would have ever been caught within a mile of that woman! She was an outcast, a social leper, and a pariah. But consider this from the thinking of his day: if Jesus truly wanted to change the world, he picked the absolute worst person with whom to do it. From the text, one can find at least five reasons Jesus should have avoided the stranger.

Strike One: She Was a Samaritan (4:9)

Those who have studied the Scriptures know well the hatred that the Jewish leaders held for the Samaritans. In the eighth century before Christ, the Assyrian army captured the ten northern tribes. Prophets such as Isaiah had warned of the impending slavery, but Israel had ignored his pleas. Around 721 B.C., the Assyrians captured the northern sections of the Holy Land and, with a swift army, reduced the children of God to dust. The mighty warriors were killed, and the young children were made servants. Yet the Assyrians had one unique atrocity in store for the vanquished Israelites: *they left some healthy Israelite women behind*. They left them there in the land of their former freedom. The purpose was simple—the women were forced to marry the godless Assyrian men. Then there were poor people, unwanted even then, who were also left behind. And they too intermarried with nonbelievers—non-Israelites.

The children produced from these unholy unions? Samaritans. The term means "half-breeds."

By the time Jesus walked the earth, the Jews carried a deep and abiding hatred for the Samaritans. It would not be an overstatement to say that they loathed even to speak of them. The Samaritans were reminders of their former captivity. To the Jews, the Samaritans were unclean, unholy, and untouchable.

If a Jew were to touch Samaritan soil on his way to Jerusalem for the holy days, he was regarded as unclean, and he was required to enter the ceremonial baptismal font (the *miqvah*) again. If a priest were to come in contact with a Samaritan, he could not serve in the temple rituals. The Samaritans were the equivalent of India's untouchables and lepers; they were deemed almost subhuman.

Yet we find Jesus not only meeting the Samaritan woman at the well, but also engaging her in conversation. He offered her "living water." He met her at her well of need.

Strike Two: She Was a Woman

When the disciples returned from their trip into the city for food, no one dared ask Jesus why he was speaking to a woman, but they certainly *thought* it. Look at John 4:27. They were confused. Why was Jesus speaking to a *woman*?

In a time when women could not own property, serve in government, or participate in civic affairs, why was Jesus bothering to speak to a *woman*? In that day, women were treated with the same contempt as cattle. *Jesus,* they must have thought, *if you are going to bring your kingdom to any fruition, why are you bothering with a woman?*

Strike Three: She Was Poor

Please notice the woman's response to Jesus in John 4:15. She said, "Sir, give me this water so that I won't get thirsty and have to keep coming here to draw water." The rich had slaves to get the water. The middle class sent their children. The poor had to get the water themselves. This woman was poor.

In the northern kingdom, the entire region was built around Mount Gerizim. It was at the foot of this mountain that Jacob originally built the well. By the time of Jesus, every person in the area had to come to this well to draw the drinkable water; and it still exists today. Every single day, this woman would place her water pot on her head and walk to the mountain to draw water from the well. The language of the text indicates that it was quite a journey for her. She did not have children to get the water or slaves to send. She had to make the arduous journey herself.

Certainly, you could have heard the apostles reasoning with Jesus, "Lord, if you want to reach the world, why are you speaking to this impoverished woman? Find a rich benefactor or a wealthy businessman! Do not waste your time with someone who obviously has nothing to give."

Yet Jesus offered her not only living water, but the type of living water that would spring up to eternal life!

Strike Four: She Was Divorced

It seems a strange turn to the conversation, doesn't it? In the middle of a discourse concerning living water, Jesus all of a sudden stopped the conversation and told the woman to "go, get your husband and bring him here." Yet perhaps it was not as strange as it sounds. Perhaps Jesus was making a point to which we should pay attention.

Sheepishly, the woman responded, "I have no husband." Jesus retorted, "You have answered correctly. You have no husband. In fact, you have had five husbands."

The woman was obviously alarmed. "Sir," she replied, "I perceive that You are a prophet. . . ." It was the equivalent of a mea culpa. She was saying, "You got me. You know me." Jesus had her dead to rights. In fact, she was so shocked by his perception that when she ran to her city fathers, she said, "Come see the man who has told me everything that I have done. Can this man be the Christ?"

Despite her spotty marital track record, Jesus continued to speak to her. He even made a clear declaration of his divinity to her when he said, "I am the Messiah," in response to her question (John 4:26).

Is it not the same today? Don't some still respond in the same way? Although divorce may be accepted, it is always difficult. But even if a church ministers to and accepts divorced persons, the social implications of going through divorce can still disrupt or even shred the church's social fabric. In many cases, one or the other or even both divorced persons end up leaving a church because of painful memories and awkward encounters with friends and family. Imagine the furor this woman could cause. Whispers would buzz like bees as she entered the sanctuary. With apologies to Nathaniel Hawthorne, I believe many of our churches still look for a *new* Scarlet Letter, whether it is the letter *D* for "divorced" or even "disruptive." While divorce does not carry the social stigma it once did, it still can devastate persons' lives.

When my mother became a Christian in 1991, she had already endured a difficult divorce. Our father blamed our mother for the conversion of their three sons to Christianity. The long, drawn-out court proceedings were painful, excruciatingly so. The only pain I witnessed that was worse than the human tug-of-war that ensued between my parents was the scorn heaped upon my mother as a divorcée. That was true even in the church. Yet Jesus, knowing this woman's history, continued to minister to her.

Strike Five: She Was Living in Sin at That Moment

Notice the second half of Jesus' statement in John 4:18. He said, "And the man you now have is not your husband." Ponder that sentence a moment. This woman, perhaps burned over her past failed relationships, had stopped marrying the men with whom she had relations. She was now *living in sin!* The fact that she came to the well at a time of day when no one else was there points to her isolation and status as an outcast, even among her own people.

In making this simple point, I ask my students this question: how many lost people consider you a friend?

Notice I do not ask, "How many lost people know your name?" or "How many lost people have you confronted?" I ask, "How many lost people consider you a friend?"

> *How many lost people consider you a friend?*

How many people in your circle of influence, who do not know Jesus, would come to you in confidence? How many non-Christians would trust you with a secret pain or problem? How many non-Christians view you not as a hunter who has them in your sights but as a confidant?

19

"Touch Not the Unclean!"

One of the clear marks of unhealthy and unbalanced Christianity is an aversion to the very mission to which Christ calls us. Persons with a toxic faith loathe contact with broken, hurting, and sinful people. Instead, they measure their holiness by their distance from the unclean and unholy people of this world. They may even view your contact with sinners as a compromise of your morals rather than an evangelistic effort. They immediately question your motives. They call you a sinner as well.

Jesus Offers the Detox: Matthew 9:12-13

Ponder Jesus' response to this particular toxic type of faith: "On hearing this, Jesus said, 'It is not the healthy who need a doctor, but the sick. But go and learn what this means: 'I desire mercy, not sacrifice.' For I have not come to call the righteous, but sinners" (Matthew 9:12-13).

He noted that his mission, and by proxy, our mission, was to go directly to unclean people. In fact, those people who think they are well do not want to see a doctor. Ironically, they are often the most ill because they are also self-deluded into thinking they are *well*.

We often skip right over the second sentence Jesus spoke in the text: "Go and learn." In those three simple words, Jesus offered the answer to their poisonous strain of faith—get out of the Holy Huddle and see the world for which he died. For the self-pious, the cure is often more painful than the disease. The disease of their comfort is disturbed by coming in contact with those who do not have comfort, yet that is our call and our mission.

Jesus' Final Words: Change Your Heart

Fulfilling our call and mission calls for more than merely a change in lifestyle; it must be a change of heart. If a few recalcitrant Christians reach out to their communities, they may change their actions, but they will not have a change of heart. Jesus concluded that a change of heart comes from becoming a person of mercy rather than just taking action ("sacrifice"). Through these actions, God, in good grace, reaches into the heart of the person who is reaching out. No one can change his or her heart alone. Compassion, just like gentleness, faithfulness, or kindness, is a gift of the Spirit. Acts of mercy are for more than the person receiving mercy; they are for the person extending mercy.

In the proper context, sacrifices are acceptable only if they come from a Christian who is merciful, not judgmental. True faith refuses to accept any concept of the "untouchables." The sinners with whom Jesus fellowshipped were the hurting and broken, and he said he came to heal them. The only true healing comes from reaching them with salvation in Jesus Christ. But that healing will touch all of us as well. As we faithfully reach out, we become conformed to the image of Christ, as Paul reminded us in Romans 12:1-8.

To whom will the broken turn when their world falls apart? As Scripture always teaches, our sinful decisions will eventually come back to haunt us, and our choices can cause a meltdown in our lives. To whom shall we turn?

Do people turn to someone who ignores them? No. Do people seek advice from the person who beats them over the head with a fifty-pound Bible? Absolutely not. They will turn only to someone with whom they feel comfortable—someone who will offer them living water.

CHAPTER THREE

The Great Pretenders

Then John's disciples came and asked him, "How is it that we
and the Pharisees fast, but your disciples do not fast?" Jesus
answered, "How can the guests of the bridegroom mourn while
he is with them? The time will come when the bridegroom will
be taken from them; then they will fast. No one sews a patch of
unshrunk cloth on an old garment, for the patch will pull away
from the garment, making the tear worse. Neither do men pour
new wine into old wineskins. If they do, the skins will burst, the
wine will run out and the wineskins will be ruined. No, they
pour new wine into new wineskins, and both are preserved."
(Matthew 9:14-17)

A Lowlife at High Tea

I *hate* cucumbers and I have a reason. Does that sound insensi-
tive or extreme? Perhaps I need to rephrase that statement.

I loathe cucumbers.

I cannot stand cucumbers.

I despise cucumbers.

I shudder at the mere smell of cucumbers.

Is that better? Perhaps you will sympathize if I explain the
situation.

About fifteen years ago, I was working for a very kind Christian
family. As part of my employment, I drove them to the airport, carried luggage, and even hung ornaments on their Christmas tree. It
was the perfect job because I have always admired them and just
being close to them enabled me to grow spiritually and intellectu-
ally. The hours of the job enabled me to complete my studies in
seminary, and the benefits far outweighed the challenges.

In fact, because of my job, I was able to travel places that I never would have seen. One particular June, we were in Houston for a convention, and the wife for whom I worked invited me to one of the most elegant restaurants in the United States. It was more like a country club than a restaurant, complete with a myriad of servants, requisite valet parking, sparkling crystal, and polished brass everywhere.

The day before we went, she reminded me not to eat that morning because I was going to experience a meal like I had never had. The morning of the meal, I awoke early and pressed my shirt. I made sure my tie was in a perfect Windsor knot. I was ready for the dining experience of a lifetime.

At the appointed hour, I picked up my host, and we drove to the most exquisite restaurant I have ever seen. Dark, rich leather covered the furniture. A woman played the harp on the landing. Waiters dressed in crisp black tuxedos rushed quietly about the restaurant. Chandeliers of pure crystal dangled gracefully above us as we were escorted to her friends who awaited our arrival. I was about to experience my first high tea.

You have to understand. On a good day I stand six feet tall and weigh 250 pounds. I am a large, uncoordinated, and clumsy guy. I can knock over a glass of iced tea from across the room. I have broken plates in restaurants by simply piling food on them at a buffet. There is a reason I had never attended a high tea.

Furthermore, I eat enough for three people. My idea of heaven is a buffet featuring fried foods and desserts. I have never met a fried food product that I did not like. If you deep-fried a rock, I would get through half of it before I even noticed. Ask anyone in my office at Liberty University. My motto for lunch is: *I would rather have bad food quickly than have to wait for good food.*

Suffice it to say, I have an unsophisticated and unrefined palate. I should never attend a high tea.

On this fateful day, I entered the dining room, which looked like a large living room. There were no tables in sight. Everyone was seated on these beautifully upholstered sofas, whispering. I was sure they were talking about me.

A waiter appeared from the mist and presented us with a large wooden box, filled with a variety of teas the likes of which I had never seen. There were teas from countries that I did not know existed! Each person picked their favorite tea, and my host picked the flavor she felt I should have. That was very gracious on her part because it saved me the embarrassment of mispronouncing the words on the labels.

When the tea arrived on platters of fine, glistening china, I intently watched each person gently hold the cup as the waiter poured the hot water. At that moment I discovered that I was the *only man* in the room who was seated. This was a high tea where apparently men were not allowed. Either that, or no other man wanted to attend.

My first dilemma arose when I searched for someplace to set my tea, but found none. All the women were gingerly resting the cups and saucers on their knees. I have never done *anything* gingerly. This was going to be a challenge. I was also half starved, having skipped breakfast and lunch for this midday event.

A few minutes later, I was firmly ensconced in a discussion that was clearly above my pay scale. The women were talking about stocks and bonds, houses and vacations, and I had nothing to contribute. I believe I had about eighty dollars to my name at the time, and that included the stray change scattered in my couch as well as the value of the couch itself.

Then like David Copperfield, the waiter appeared again. He was scaring me; he always approached as if out of thin air. He wheeled in a cart, on which sat a multitiered server with plates. The plates were loaded down with food, and I looked around and saw women eating sandwiches. My heart began to race as finally I anticipated a meal.

These were sandwiches—tiny, quartered sandwiches with the crusts cut off. Between the slices of the quartered, tiny, crustless white bread? Cucumbers. More specifically, thin slices of cucumbers with cream cheese filling. There was no meat to be found. I am sure some readers are philosophical vegetarians, but I am a committed carnivore. For me to enjoy what I am eating, it has to have had a face and a parent.

I was dejected but not yet defeated. After the women took their quarter slices and rested them on their knees, I thanked the waiter, took eight or nine of the small sandwiches, and pressed them together. As I raised my cucumber sub to my mouth, my eyes met the eyes of my host, who was clearly not pleased. She leaned over and whispered to me, "You have just made a forty-dollar sandwich." Out of the corner of my eye I caught the waiter laughing. It was mortifying.

My humiliation was not yet complete. During the course of the next thirty minutes, I juggled the cup and saucer on one knee and my plate of cucumber sandwiches on the other knee, with little success. The women cast sideways glances at me but graciously tried not to laugh as I spilled my tea a couple of times and dropped my sandwiches once. I even managed to get cream cheese on my tie—the one with the perfect Windsor knot.

By the end of the meal, I simply wanted to crawl under the cart and disappear. I was embarrassed beyond belief, having failed my first (and only) attempt at mixing with high society. I was also quite tired. Keeping up appearances is *exhausting*.

Fear and Loathing in New Jerusalem

I am not for one second suggesting that the benevolent woman who brought me to the high tea was putting on airs. Neither were any of her friends. I can state without any fear of contradiction that *I was*. I was trying with all my might to be something *I was not*. I was a textbook case of lifestyle hypocrisy. I was the perfect picture of the disingenuous and the fake. I was trying so hard to fit into a mold that I could not fit into that I was draining my energy and patience. If there was a lesson to be learned from my adventure, it was that I was not destined to make it in high society.

I was being a toxic pharisee and my poison was cucumbers.

The question asked of Jesus in Matthew 9:14-17 was actually not asked by any of the religious leaders. It was asked by the followers of John the Baptist. However, the religious leaders were guilty of a form of showboat faith, where personal devotion was prominently placed on public display. In fact, Jesus launched into such an indictment of them in Matthew 6:16-18 that it presents us with one of the firm principles of genuine Christianity: outward fasting without inner faith is an utter failure.

> *Outward fasting without inner faith is an utter failure.*

The Gospels are full of examples of the hypocritical nature of people who proclaimed themselves as

26

religious. Jesus himself strongly condemned the type of poisonous faith that stresses outward obedience over inner devotion. This faith is a clear symptom of toxic Christians who contaminate others. For example, Jesus stated, "Beware of the scribes, who desire to go around in long robes, [and] love greetings in the marketplaces, the best seats in the synagogues, and the best places at feasts, who devour widows' houses, and for a pretense make long prayers. These will receive greater condemnation" (Mark 12:38-40 NKJV).

Do you notice a pattern in their deception? Pay close attention to Jesus' words.

1. *Toxic faith parades its holiness.* They "go around in long robes." The scribes, who were the seminary professors and theologians of their day, wore robes that identified themselves as such. The robe itself was a distinguishing uniform that demanded favor and respect.

2. *Toxic faith anticipates adulation.* They "love greetings in the marketplaces," which were a sign of popularity. If they existed today, the scribes would only greet people at their own book signings. The "greeting" was a sign of human praise.

3. *Toxic faith enjoys being seen.* They take "the best seats," as if there is a hierarchy in our faith. The best seat was not just the most comfortable, but it was also the most visible.

4. *Toxic faith enjoys special benefits.* They have the "best places at feasts." They always insisted on sitting at the table of honor, or the speakers' table. They were served first at these communal feasts, even though, ironically, the feasts were designed to show the equality of everyone as a brother or a sister in the Lord.

5. *Toxic faith shows no mercy.* They "devour widows' houses." This act of foreclosure betrayed their public statements of personal mercy. Like vultures, they feasted on the flock. This type of Christian shows mercy just as long as it does not cost him or her, but when there is a profit to be made, mercy is tossed aside and the homes are taken.

6. *Toxic faith loves the sound of its own voice.* They "make long prayers." This is known in common parlance as showing off. They used long words, complicated and obscure citations, and flowery language to make sure people were impressed. Ultimately, Jesus was illustrating that they were praying for the audience, not the Lord God.

Welcome to My Pity Party

Jesus' admonition was toward a genuine and authentic faith that concentrated only on devotion to God. It was in direct opposition to the Pharisaical method of public displays. With regard to prayer, John's disciples were questioning the private devotion of his followers, but only because they did not see the apostles making a public exhibition of it. Jesus had addressed this earlier when he preached the Sermon on the Mount, also in Galilee:

> When you fast, do not be like the hypocrites, with a sad countenance. For they disfigure their faces that they may appear to men to be fasting. Assuredly, I say to you, they have their reward. But you, when you fast, anoint your head and wash your face, so that you do not appear to men to be fasting, but to your Father who is in the secret place; and your Father who sees in secret will reward you openly. (Matthew 6:16-18 NKJV)

The Pharisees made quite a spectacle of themselves when they fasted. They marked the two fasting days each week by not shaving or bathing, and by eliciting sympathy from every person with whom they came in contact. They made a special effort to let everyone know how much they were "suffering" by acting miserable. It was a public pity party.

Jesus did not negate the power of fasting, but he focused our attention on the only important purpose of fasting—it is an intensely personal act of extreme devotion that shows God that even the essential things in life (such as food) are not as important as the eternal things.

Why do toxic Christians make such a public display of their faith? Have you ever experienced the following? When you encounter such persons, they immediately let you know how holy they are and will do so in casual conversation. For instance:

- They always remind you in conversation of their three prayer times each day.
- They casually let you know that they memorized the book of Jeremiah, just this morning.
- They remind you in conversation that they are going to church for the eleventh time this week because the pastor *needs* them.

- They tell you they are personal friends of some famous Christian because they are so strong spiritually.

Even preachers can become subject to this toxin. As evangelist Junior Hill so wisely states, those types of preachers love their own sermons so much that after they finish them, they sign their own Bibles!

The ultimate question, however, remains: *why* do they do this? They do this because it is symptomatic of a central premise of toxic faith: their faith needs to be recognized for them to feel spiritual. Private spirituality demands nothing except intimacy with God, but hypocritical Christians need to be recognized as being holy. So, to test whether you are susceptible, let me ask you a diagnostic question: if they gave you a medal for being humble, would you wear it?

The Other Side of Humble: Holiness by Comparison

There is another method of this toxic form of faith. Some Christians infected with this disease employ a variation of false humility. They out-holy you specifically. By this I mean they find some way to show you how

> *If they gave you a medal for being humble, would you wear it?*

weak your faith is and by comparison how strong their faith is. This is known as holiness by comparison.

An appropriate example is found in Jesus' parable in Luke 18. He began by introducing two hypothetical people: a tax collector and a Pharisee. The Pharisee was obsessed with this holiness by comparison and even began his prayer in the temple by thanking God that he was better than other people: "The Pharisee stood and prayed thus with himself, 'God, I thank You that I am not like other men—extortioners, unjust, adulterers, or even as this tax collector. I fast twice a week; I give tithes of all that I possess'" (Luke 18:11-12 NKJV). It would be laughable if it were not so tragic and so true. The Pharisee stood and prayed aloud that he was not like the other people who obviously were so much more sinful than he was.

Then Jesus continued, "And the tax collector, standing afar off, would not so much as raise his eyes to heaven, but beat his breast, saying, 'God, be merciful to me a sinner!' " (Luke 18:13 NKJV). The tax collector, among the most hated in all of Israel, did not make such a show of his prayer. In fact, Jesus stated that he stood at a distance because he did not feel worthy of standing in God's presence. He was penitent, as illustrated by the beating of his chest. He was sickened by his lack of holiness. Yet Jesus concluded, "I tell you, this man went down to his house justified rather than the other; for everyone who exalts himself will be humbled [put down], and he who humbles himself will be exalted" (Luke 18:14 NKJV). The application is explicit: humility is a private virtue that is infinitely greater than the public flaunting of pseudoholiness.

Throwing You under the Church Bus (or Car)

Why would the pharisee go to such great lengths to attempt to trump you in acts of public holiness? Why do such toxic people delight in showing you how holy they are? The answer is simple: when toxic Christians belittle your devotion, they think it makes their life easier. They don't have to be close to God as long as they look closer to God than you are.

> *When toxic Christians belittle your devotion, they think it makes their life easier. They don't have to be close to God as long as they look closer to God than you are.*

It is deluded and deceptive thinking, but it is consistently one reason cited why people do not go to church. The self-righteous people make them feel vilified for even trying to draw near to God.

Authentic faith does not live in comparison to other Christians.

Authentic faith lives in comparison only with its own past.

You may not be the strongest Christian in your church, but let me ask you: *is your faith stronger than it was before?* This is the only comparison that matters. When others seek to compare themselves to you and disparage you, they are only attempting to spread their toxin. Do not let their insecurity affect your devotion.

You cannot live your faith in comparison to others.

When I first became the president of the seminary at Liberty University, a sweet older woman at our church pulled me aside after service one Sunday and gently chided me about my vehicle.

"Honey," she said, "now that you are in the administration, you need to get a better car. Your truck does not fit the office you will hold. People will be watching."

Truthfully, my truck was not the prettiest vehicle in the parking lot. It was an old 1976 Ford F-100 pickup truck, bright yellow, with dents along both sides. I had purchased it cheaply, but it ran beautifully and it served the purpose of getting me to the school. She pointed out that others drove cars that were much more distinguished.

I felt sheepish and self-conscious about my truck, but I knew that I would not be happy with a luxury automobile. As illustrated by the opening story, it is not easy for me to get my body into a compact car. However, I relented and purchased a 1999 Ford Explorer with four-wheel drive. It had no dents and looked more presentable than the old truck.

Still, the conversation haunted me. She did not mean any harm whatsoever by her statement, but I knew that I had made a decision based solely on appearance. In short, the Explorer was not *me*. I was being disingenuous, which was the very thing against which I preached. I was as bad as the Pharisee who fasted for show.

Then a friend approached me after church one day. He told me that my SUV looked like it did not fit me. He stated that I am such an overt personality, I needed a vehicle to match. He asked for the keys, and I handed them over to him, wondering what he was going to do.

A month later, he returned my Explorer. He had lifted it several inches and placed twenty-two-inch rims on the wheels. The students call this "rolling on dubs." The SUV had running lights all down the side, with stripes brightly painted to match. He had bolted a 3200-watt speaker box in the back and installed new lights all around it.

I doubt if there is a seminary president in the world who drives such a vehicle. I am sure most would be embarrassed to even be seen in it. However, I absolutely love it. And in fulfillment of that sweet lady's prophecy, people now know when I have arrived! I am sure there are people even on the campus who get uncomfortable when I drive up.

The point is, as much as I want to be like those other men of God that I emulate, I can only be myself. God designed me to be the best me that I can be, not by comparison to others but in sanctification to being like God. I am called to be the most devoted follower of Christ I can be; and in comparison to what I once was, I am slowly getting there. It is not a race with others, and it is not a parade or show.

Ultimately, I am called to please God and serve people. I am accountable to those above me, and so I asked my chancellor and the president of Liberty University, Jerry Falwell Jr., if the gaudy SUV was an impediment to my office. He just laughed and said he would be disappointed if I changed it in any way.

At the end of the day, I am called to please God and serve my leaders by doing the best job that I can. I can accomplish this only with authentic faith and genuine Christianity.

CHAPTER FOUR

How Dare You Help?

At that time Jesus went through the grainfields on the Sabbath. His disciples were hungry and began to pick some heads of grain and eat them. When the Pharisees saw this, they said to him, "Look! Your disciples are doing what is unlawful on the Sabbath."

He answered, "Haven't you read what David did when he and his companions were hungry? He entered the house of God, and he and his companions ate the consecrated bread—which was not lawful for them to do, but only for the priests. Or haven't you read in the Law that on the Sabbath the priests in the temple desecrate the day and yet are innocent? I tell you that one greater than the temple is here. If you had known what these words mean, 'I desire mercy, not sacrifice,' you would not have condemned the innocent. For the Son of Man is Lord of the Sabbath." (Matthew 12:1-13)

The Sin of Sweatpants

Soccer practice had been difficult. Actually, that is an understatement. Soccer practice had been an exercise in torture management. Our coach was especially gifted at extracting every iota of energy out of his players during practice—running wind sprints until we were dragging ourselves from the field, sprinting up the stairs of the football stadium until we were crying, doing push-ups until I was lying on the ground, praying for death or at least a medical condition that would get me out of there.

It was summer, and the two-a-days had begun. During the heat of summer, we were practicing both morning and afternoon, and we rarely touched a soccer ball. Instead, we were apparently training for some marathon that existed only in our coach's head. Even now, twenty-five years later, I break out into a sweat thinking about it. I am guessing that somewhere, one of my coaches is sitting in a retirement home, making the other patients do thirty laps around the nurses' station.

However, after I showered, I managed to get into my car and drive to church. We were having vacation Bible school that week, and I had volunteered to work with the fifth-grade boys. Secretly, I was probably more excited about the event than the kids I was going to help, since this was my first VBS ever. I was a relatively young Christian, and I felt as if I had missed out on a lifetime of flannel graphs, cheap Kool-Aid, and Hydrox cookies. As I pulled into the church's gravel parking lot, I was whistling one of those infernal VBS songs we had learned. Those songs haunted me in my sleep.

I did not have time to go home and change, and I was walking up the sidewalk to our church in shorts and a Gahanna Lincoln High School T-shirt. Little did I know that I was going to run into McGruff the Christian Crime Dog.

He usually lurked at the entrance of the church. Though I did not know his actual age, I always assumed he was a charter member of our church. In retrospect, he may have been a charter member of the church in Jerusalem. He probably passed out bulletins at Pentecost. In all the years I knew this gentleman, I never saw him smile. He was always at the church but was never happy. He served as the leader of the Cold Water Committee. He was easily a foot taller than I was. But he seemed even taller, since every time I saw him, he blocked out the sun.

As I attempted to open the door to the church, he abruptly grabbed my hand.

"Young man, where are you going?" he asked.

I said something about going to my classroom to make sure it was ready for the crafts. This particular evening we were going to make our own apostle puppets with paper sandwich bags. We were even going to glue on cotton balls for beards.

"Not in those clothes!" he huffed. "I don't know where you were raised, but when you come to church, you do *not* wear shorts."

He was leaning down to emphasize the point, and his face was mere inches from mine. Apparently, he had eaten a tuna sandwich for lunch.

"But I came straight from soccer practice," I stated, "and I didn't have time to go home."

"Well, you march yourself right back home and put on respectable clothing to wear when you come to God's house!" The last consonant of the word *house* sounded like a snake's hiss to me. I knew it was a fight I was not going to win.

So I went home that night.

And I never returned all week.

The next Sunday, I did not have to tell my partner in the class why I was absent. He came up to me apologetically and whispered that he had heard about my encounter with McGruff. Apparently, so did our pastor because that morning, he preached from Matthew 12. Read the text and see if you can guess what my wonderful pastor was trying to say to our congregation.

Introduction: Broken Grain and Broken Laws

Ironic, isn't it? At the end of Matthew 11, Jesus had just finished saying these words: "Come to me, all you who are weary and burdened, and I will give you rest. Take my yoke upon you and learn from me, for I am gentle and humble in heart, and you will find rest for your souls. For my yoke is easy and my burden is light" (vv. 28-30).

Jesus had not yet begun to walk through the Galilean fields when the Pharisees jumped at the opportunity to try to trap him. As his disciples were passing through the wheat fields, they grabbed some of the tops of wheat stalks. Rubbing the wheat vigorously in their hands, they separated the wheat germ from the husks, and they used the wheat somewhat like many people use sunflower seeds—a quick snack for energy.

After the end of the Old Testament period, during the four-hundred-year interval between Malachi and Matthew, the religious leaders developed quite a litany of rules concerning the Sabbath. These rules were not found in the Scriptures, but they were added into a collection of commentaries on daily life, known as the *Mishnah*. The word literally means the "repetition," and the collection, which began around 150 years before Christ, was completed around A.D. 200. Eventually, this collection, covering all dilemmas of life, was separated into six huge sections. The section on actions during the Sabbath, known as *Kodashim*, is the relevant one here. The rules for the Sabbath included the restriction on cooking, bathing, speaking, and working. In fact, a devout Pharisee was allowed to walk only a quarter day's journey on the Sabbath, and that was to and from worship.

The Sadducees rejected these oral laws, but the Pharisees held to them to an extreme degree. It was a criminal offense to break any of these rules, and often the Pharisees employed non-Jews to monitor the Jews' adherence to the rules. The Pharisees claimed that Jesus was breaking the Sabbatical laws by allowing his disciples to eat the grain for which they had to work.

Did the Disciples Sin by Eating on the Sabbath?

So the question remains: did Jesus allow the disciples to sin? Did they violate the Scripture by rubbing their hands together (working) to get to the wheat germ? Or were the Pharisees objecting to the disciples taking wheat that was not theirs? Were Peter, James, Andrew, and the rest of the followers stealing grain from a random farmer?

They were not guilty of theft. Deuteronomy 23:25 (NKJV) states, "When you come into your neighbor's standing grain, you may pluck the heads with your hand, but you shall not use a sickle on your neighbor's standing grain." In an agrarian society, people who walked through countless farms as they walked from town to town could take handfuls of grain for sustenance, but they could not harvest huge amounts from someone else's farm.

They were not guilty of working on the Sabbath. Jesus answered the Pharisees in Matthew 12:3-4 by citing David's experience (1 Samuel 21:1-6). David arrived in Nob, just north of Jerusalem, with his soldiers. On official business, they were hungry when they approached the priest. David asked for food, but the priest said he had no food that was edible by the common man. All he had was showbread, which had been consecrated before God to be eaten only by the priests.

David responded that *all* bread is common. The only thing that made the bread sacred was that it had been offered for the priests (1 Samuel 21:5). The priest therefore gave David and his men the bread, even though it had been dedicated for another purpose.

They were not guilty of breaking the Sabbath. Jesus followed up with another example (Matthew 12:5). He observed that the priests worked on the Sabbath, didn't they? Yet that work did not make them sinful because it had a holy purpose. In the Gospel of John, Jesus gave a parallel defense by citing a priest performing a circumcision on the Sabbath (John 7:22-24).

The Sabbath: From Refreshment to Restriction

The finality of Jesus' indictment could not have been more incisive. He concluded his condemnation of the Pharisees by putting the Sabbath in proper perspective. He said, "I tell you that one greater than the temple is here. If you had known what these words mean, 'I desire mercy, not sacrifice,' you would not have condemned the innocent. For the Son of Man is Lord of the Sabbath" (Matthew 12:6-8).

Do you see the paradox in Jesus' words? The Sabbath had been established to bring refreshment to the children of God, and the Pharisees had turned it into a legalistic smorgasbord of crimes, rules, and regulations. Yet it is precisely this point that illustrates one of the major indictments against toxic Christians: toxic Christians embrace obedience over mercy.

Perhaps it might be better to say it this way—they would rather have mindless obedience than thoughtful mercy toward others. They would rather follow the letter of the Law than the spirit of the Law. Does this sound like anyone you know? God established the Sabbath as a celebration of the end of God's creative work (Genesis 2:1-3). It was designed to be a break from normal pursuits to find refreshment in celebrating God.

> *Toxic Christians embrace obedience over mercy.*

I often tell my students that there is a book that I could never write because it would surely get me fired. It would be titled *I Never Had a Sabbath.* Think about it. The day we set aside to relax and celebrate the Lord is the busiest day of my ministerial life!

Going to meetings, working with committees, teaching, preaching, setting up, tearing down, planning, organizing, and leading all play into the normal Sunday.

Not much rest involved on my Sabbath at church.

However, the Pharisees decided to turn the refreshment in God into human restrictions. Instead of being free worship, it was enforced obedience. The rules were enforced with an iron hand. It reminds me of the worship leader who becomes frustrated with the lackluster singing in his congregation one Sunday and screams from the pulpit, "You people had better *praise louder*, or I am coming out there to shake you awake!"

Jesus Responds: Playing the Game of Gotcha (Matthew 12:9-13)

Jesus did not stop with the disciples' quick meal. He actually walked into the synagogue. The Pharisees felt that they had a perfect opportunity to nail Jesus on their Sabbath rules. Knowing that Jesus had healed people, they asked him if he could do it on the Sabbath. They felt it was an unwinnable situation for him. If Jesus did heal someone, he would be guilty of breaking the *Mishnah* rules. If Jesus did not heal someone, he would be seen as cold and heartless.

In the parallel passage in the Gospel of Mark, the Bible states that the question incited anger in Jesus because he saw the calculating and manipulative hearts of the religious leaders (3:5). It was not a sudden impulse, like rash and uncontrolled rage, in our Lord. It was Jesus' firm disposition against the hypocrisy of the Pharisees. It was his righteous response to empty religion. Being angry without sin is possible, as noted in Ephesians 4:26. Notice Jesus' response to their challenge:

> Going on from that place, he went into their synagogue, and a man with a shriveled hand was there. Looking for a reason to accuse Jesus, they asked him, "Is it lawful to heal on the Sabbath?" He said to them, "If any of you has a sheep and it falls into a pit on the Sabbath, will you not take hold of it and lift it out? How much more valuable is a man than a sheep! Therefore it is lawful to do good on the Sabbath." Then he said to the man,

"Stretch out your hand." So he stretched it out and it was completely restored, just as sound as the other.

Jesus healed the man and called him to stand, breaking yet another rule of the Pharisees. In so doing, Jesus cemented the central rule that is supposed to guide us in our Christian ethic: it is lawful to "do good" on the Sabbath. It is an act of mercy, which is the purpose of obedience.

The Saddest Proof of Toxic Faith

One would imagine that a healing in the synagogue would make the service quite exciting. Could you imagine if that happened in front of everyone in your church next Sunday? Certainly, it would add a measure of electricity that could not be duplicated by a program, wouldn't it?

Yet the response of the Pharisees is disheartening: "The Pharisees went out and plotted how they might kill Jesus" (Matthew 12:14). Instead of being thrilled that a man with a withered hand was healed, they were infuriated. The Bible adds that the Pharisees were "filled with rage" (Luke 6:11 NKJV). Mark 3:6 (NKJV) notes that the Pharisees joined together with their political enemies for the sole purpose of trying to "destroy Him."

The Symptoms of Toxic Christians

In the fall of 1988, a small revival broke out at my college campus. The Ministerial Association of Cumberland College had invited a local pastor to preach from Monday through Wednesday in the chapel. The planning was not spectacular. There were no posters. The word of mouth was not particularly extraordinary.

Yet God was gracious to visit the campus that week.

One evening, the service went until almost 11:00 p.m. The altar was full with students getting right with God. It was one of those services that lingers in your mind for years. The aisles were so full with students praying that you could not find room to walk.

Yet the spiritual stillness of the hour was broken by the night janitor, who walked into the back of the auditorium and exclaimed, "Y'all quit this mess now. You can finish this stuff tomorrow. Go . . . to . . . bed!"

Do you know anyone who would respond like this? Think about it. Do you know people who respond with anger when revival breaks out in church? The symptoms are quite distinct. They can never celebrate when victory comes to someone else, either because of jealousy or because of control. They never seem to be happy, even in the midst of a glorious triumph.

An old adage says, "A pessimist knows the cost of everything but the value of nothing." Pessimists never see the blessing because their minds are fixed on the bottom line. They consider the price of spiritual victory to be too steep:

- Services will go too long.
- New people mean added costs.
- This will never last.
- Someone else will take control of this.
- Who do these people think they are?
- This was not part of the planned service.

I am sure you can add to this list, and it could fill a book all by itself. Toxic faith is a faith that would rather see order than power. Order refers to their prescribed direction, not the biblical sense of decorum. It is an issue of control.

Yet Jesus embraced the spontaneous acts of mercy rather than ritualistic obedience. Since he designed the Law and the Sabbath, do you not think that his interpretation of them should be the guiding principle? When you encounter toxic Christians, especially when you are walking with God, your response will be the same as his—righteous indignation. Yet you should not do anything rash. Do what Jesus did. Respond with firmness and the word, speak the truth in love, and do not let them dissuade you from being an agent of mercy.

CHAPTER FIVE
Signs, Signs, Everywhere Are Signs

*Then some of the Pharisees and teachers of the law said to him,
"Teacher, we want to see a miraculous sign from you." He
answered, "A wicked and adulterous generation asks for a miraculous sign! But none will be given it except the sign of the
prophet Jonah. For as Jonah was three days and three nights in
the belly of a huge fish, so the Son of Man will be three days and
three nights in the heart of the earth. The men of Nineveh will
stand up at the judgment with this generation and condemn it;
for they repented at the preaching of Jonah, and now one greater
than Jonah is here. The Queen of the South will rise at the judgment with this generation and condemn it; for she came from the
ends of the earth to listen to Solomon's wisdom, and now one
greater than Solomon is here. When an evil spirit comes out of a
man, it goes through arid places seeking rest and does not find it.
Then it says, 'I will return to the house I left.' When it arrives, it
finds the house unoccupied, swept clean and put in order. Then
it goes and takes with it seven other spirits more wicked than
itself, and they go in and live there. And the final condition of
that man is worse than the first. That is how it will be with this
wicked generation." (Matthew 12:38-45)*

Out of My Comfort; Out of My Seat

In the fall of 2007, I was the graduation speaker at Kabarak
University in Nakuru, Kenya. The chancellor of the university was
also the former president of Kenya, His Excellency Daniel Arap
Moi. In the rarefied air of speaking before presidents and kings, I
wanted to make the best presentation possible.

Having prepared diligently, I packed my best suit, made sure my graduation gown was pressed, and embarked on the journey. Though I had made numerous trips to Africa, I had never been to Kenya; and as the plane approached Nairobi, I excitedly looked out the window and marveled at the beauty.

Making the trip much more memorable was the fact that my son Braxton was accompanying me. Over the course of time, I discovered that long trips were much more enjoyable when Braxton traveled with me. Because my wife had her hands full with our three-year-old son Drake, she often allowed Braxton to travel with me. At the tender age of nine, Braxton had already traveled to Israel, the Bahamas, Canada, Amsterdam, and twenty-six states. He loves to travel as much as I do, and he was happily reading the travel books along with me.

We have a number of intractable rules by which we abide when we travel together. We try not to check any baggage. We greet each person with a handshake and grace, remembering to use the words *thank you, please, ma'am,* and *sir.* Most important, we live by the mantra *roll with the punches*—whatever food we are offered, however long the worship services, or whatever the accommodations—roll with it. Never be rude to your hosts, and never refuse their hospitality.

Thankfully, neither Braxton nor I have ever balked at any food. It is not surprising for an adult, but it is quite remarkable for a boy not yet ten years old. Since he has been traveling with me, Braxton has eaten pickled herring, roast goat, bison, alligator, llama, and countless other fried meats. He has never recoiled, and he has never refused. He has eaten sushi, even though he thinks we are supposed to fish with it.

We have stayed in the Masai Mara, at the Hippo Bend River, where hippos walked beneath our cabin at night and roared. We have slept inside the Old City walls of Jerusalem during firefights. We walked among the Santeria witch doctors in the Bahamian open bazaar in Nassau. He never flinched during our outings— except once.

At the Kabarak graduation ceremony, the students of the Kabarak Academy performed a traditional African Christian song. The melodies were wonderful, and the students danced to the rhythm of the song. Dressed in their blue and gray uniforms, the students had angelic voices. Braxton was seated on the platform with me, right beside the provost of the university. The trees swayed in the breeze as the students sang and chanted the song of praise in their mother tongue.

At the chorus of the song, one young woman let loose with a yelp that pierced the sleepy afternoon air. It was part of the song, yet we were not prepared for it. It was so loud that it sounded like an approaching warrior. No one else in the crowd of hundreds moved since they were expecting it as part of the praise chorus.

No one told Braxton and me, however.

I looked over at my son, and his eyes were as wide as pie plates. He had pulled his feet onto the chair and was crouching on the seat, apparently ready to run in case something happened. His hands gripped the sides of the seat. He thought we were under attack.

For the first time, Braxton flinched. This was decidedly out of his comfort zone. It shocked him. You should have seen his facial expression. It was priceless.

Even if you have never traveled outside your county or your state, I am sure you have seen this facial expression. Just think back to a time when someone shouted, "Amen!" during the sermon. This is especially true if you attend a church where it does not often take place. If it has not happened in your church in a while, just try it one Sunday. Fifty heads spin around to see who said it. A nervous jitter rises in the room. Church leaders automatically begin planning for a business meeting to discuss it.

Or if you are feeling especially seditious, don't print the bulletin one Sunday. You will see longtime members enter the sanctuary cautiously, almost sheepishly. Like they are scouting a haunted house, they will look around to be sure they are in the right church.

It Was Not a Question; It Was a Challenge

In our study text of Matthew 12, the Pharisees did not ask a question; they presented a challenge. As Jesus was teaching at the cities along the shores of the Sea of Galilee, a demon-possessed man was brought to him. The man was so beset that he was blind and without speech. Jesus healed him, and immediately, the man could both see and speak.

The large crowd that was following Jesus actually asked the question that provoked the challenge by the Pharisees: "And all the multitudes were amazed and said, 'Could this be the Son of David?'" (Matthew 12:23 NKJV). The question was extremely important to the religious leaders because the title "Son of David" was a messianic title. The people were beginning to believe that this peripatetic teacher from Nazareth was actually the *Messiah*!

The Pharisees could not stand for this development. The next verse records that the Pharisees began to formulate a plan to answer the question. We read, "Now when the Pharisees heard it they said, 'This fellow does not cast out demons except by Beelzebub, the ruler of the demons'" (Matthew 12:24 NKJV). Along with the crowd, the Pharisees had witnessed the healing. They could not deny the veracity of the miracle, so they attributed the miracle to Jesus' being demonic rather than being sent from God. They said he was a servant of Beelzebub, a demonic worker of darkness in Philistine mythology.

The Unpardonable Sin (Matthew 12:25-37)

Jesus responded in the following moments by using simple reasoning: *how can I cast out a demon to heal a man if I am a demon and desire for people to be demon-possessed?* One would assume that since demon possession was his goal, as the Pharisees were postulating, he would be busy casting *in* demons, not exorcising them. Jesus knew what they were thinking and gave a logical response: "Jesus knew their thoughts and said to them, 'Every kingdom divided against itself will be ruined, and every city or household divided against itself will not stand. If Satan drives out Satan, he is divided against himself. How then can his kingdom stand?'" (Matthew 12:25-26).

Then our Lord went one step farther. He stated that the Pharisees, in fact, were committing the one act that would send them to hell: rejecting Jesus as the Messiah. This text, which has become known as the "unpardonable sin" discourse, has caused quite a controversy among many Christians. Jesus stated,

> Therefore I say to you, every sin and blasphemy will be forgiven men, but the blasphemy against the Spirit will not be forgiven men. Anyone who speaks a word against the Son of Man, it will be forgiven him; but whosoever speaks against the Holy Spirit, it

will not be forgiven him, either in this age or in the age to come. (Matthew 12:31-32 NKJV)

Throughout church history, much has been made of Jesus' words about the sin that cannot be forgiven. Some have taught that it is publicly denying Jesus in a crowd. Others have believed that it is saying some sort of formula of words in a certain order, blaspheming the Holy Spirit.

In the context of the passage, Jesus was responding to the argument of the Pharisees, which was in direct response to the question of the people in Matthew 12:23. The people wondered whether Jesus was the Messiah, and the Pharisees said Jesus was not the Messiah but, in fact, an agent of Satan. Jesus rebuked their plan and stated that if they rejected the Holy Spirit's conviction of their hearts to accept him, it was the only sin that damns the soul.

Jesus' public declaration of his divinity is abundantly clear in the passage. The people asked whether he was the "Son of David," a messianic title for the one who will rule on the throne in the New Jerusalem. Jesus referred to himself as the "Son of Man," the title of the one who would bring redemption (Daniel 7:13). Since his ability to perform miracles was an authentication of his nature, and the work of the Holy Spirit calls us to believe in him, the rejection of such is the denial of Christ as the only Savior.

Show Us a Sign, You Fraud! (Matthew 12:38)

The Pharisees responded to Jesus' harsh condemnation of them by attempting to trap him. They obviously did not believe in Jesus as the Christ, and neither did they believe that Jesus could *actually* perform miracles. Perhaps it was trickery? Perhaps Jesus just happened to be in the right place at the right time? It was not a request from people who wanted to believe; rather, it was a challenge from those who wanted to condemn Jesus as a fraud.

They asked for a sign, which in the Greek is *semeion*. They wanted proof because they did not believe he could produce it. In their eyes, Jesus was guilty and could not ever be proved innocent.

Even among the most conservative Christians, you will find people who believe in such works of God as divine healing. I often tell my students that I believe in divine healing, but I have trouble with some of the divine healers. Often they blame a lack of healing on the sick person's faith, which is poor theology. Imagine telling Paul that he had a thorn in the flesh because he was weak in his faith (2 Corinthians 12:7-10). Yet the challenge from the Pharisees did *not* come from their *not* having seen the miracle but from their distrust over the actual miracle itself.

Signs Are Only for Those Who Read Them (Matthew 12:39-42)

Jesus did not mock their request for proof but rather their willingness to believe the proof. He cited a story with which everyone was familiar, the story of Jonah preaching to the Ninevites.

Imagine that you are a farmer in Nineveh, working in your field and minding your own business. All of a sudden, you see a man approaching from a distance. His clothes are in tatters, and they barely cling to his gaunt frame. His hair seems to be caked with mucouslike grease and is matted beyond repair. He looks like walking death, his skin bleached and blotchy. Even before he comes near, you can smell him, an awful odor emanating from him like a garbage truck filled with rotting food.

And he is preaching! He is calling to you and telling you a horrible tale of being trapped in the belly of a fish for three solid days, until the fish spewed him out. Instead of blaming bad fortune, he is telling you that it is his fault. God told him to come and preach to the people of your country, but he refused and ran the other way. His internment in his oceanic prison was the judgment of God. "Repent!" he exclaims, "or God will find you as well!"

The audacity of Jonah's message was compounded by the fact that he was a mortal enemy of the Ninevites. The people of Nineveh had enslaved his people, and now he was coming to tell them to find peace with God!

Jesus' use of the citywide revival in Nineveh was especially poignant to the Pharisees. When the Ninevites were given a sign, the entire city of 120,000 people repented. Jonah 3:5-6 (NKJV) records: "So the people of Nineveh believed God, proclaimed a fast, and put on sackcloth, from the greatest to the least of them. Then word came to the king of Nineveh; and he arose from his throne and laid aside his robe, covered himself with sackcloth and sat in ashes."

Jesus' point must have stung the Pharisees: your hated enemies and most ruthless captors, the men of Nineveh, will stand in judgment of you. The godless warriors who slaughtered you and took your forebears captive became godly and penitent men and women. The heathens became holy—but you Pharisees will not.

The Song of the Suspicious

The most ruthless Christians you know have the same genetic flaw. The defining character trait that emanates from their very pores is that they are eternally suspicious. They will never believe.

Regardless of your testimony, they will not believe it is true.

They will question your motives, and they will doubt the results of the work of God. They sit in the middle of a revival with their arms crossed and wait for everything to fall apart. Like the Pharisees, they bring the atmosphere of worship and praise in a room to a screeching halt. In the language of my students at Liberty University, they are a "buzzkill."

Their abiding and guiding character trait? They are *inherently distrustful*. Toxic persons may have many reasons for disbelieving, but most of these reasons are justifications for their lack of faith rather than honest skepticism:

> *Toxic Christians are perpetually suspicious. Regardless of the evidence of God's work, they never believe and never get on board. They constantly criticize. They sit with dour and sour looks on their faces as God brings blessings. They are not just distrustful; they are critics of your motives, your message, and even the results. They believe God can't work.*

They refuse to believe because it is out of their comfort zone. They are used to Christianity operating in the manner to which they are accustomed. A new style has to be wrong because the way they have done things is more important to them than the results. It has to be wrong because we have never done it that way before.

They refuse to believe because someone else is getting the credit. Toxic leaders will always fight for position, even if their leadership has failed. When the new method that succeeds threatens their old method over which they have control, they react negatively and infect the whole atmosphere.

They refuse to believe because they are jealous. It is hard to believe why anyone would be angry over a revival among the children of God, but you have to look no further than the Pharisees to see why this happens. They asked for signs, not because they wanted to see any signs but because they could not perform any.

They refuse to believe because they are angry at God. Ultimately, they view anything outside their comfort zone as a threat and an insult. When a mission speaker came to our church in Colorado and spoke of the revival breaking out in India, one gentleman talked with me a few days later. "Why are we promoting other countries?" he asked. "Why not tell of the revival happening in Colorado?" I asked him what revival he was referencing, and the question angered him. He muttered something about God doing it here if God chose to do so, and he walked away.

Signs Are Everywhere, but People Who Listen Are Not

When I was doing research for this book, I had the opportunity to interview a professor at the Hebrew University in Jerusalem on Mount Scopus. He was a Jewish theologian who graciously allowed me to ask him probing questions concerning the state of modern Judaism.

I gingerly asked why some believed that a full third of modern Jews are Jewish in nationality only, not in devotion. He poignantly answered:

It is not that God is hiding from us. It is that we no longer look for [God]. It is [the] same with [God's] work among us. God is always at work, but we have stopped asking. We are surprised when God works elsewhere, but we are also a little angry. The Talmud teaches that if we keep the Sabbath, then the Sabbath will keep us. We stopped, and now we are threatened. And then we get angry.

Many Christians would concur with his assessment. Those who are in a drought often resent those who have just received rain, don't they?

CHAPTER SIX
The Dead Faith of the Living

Then some Pharisees and teachers of the law came to Jesus from Jerusalem and asked, "Why do your disciples break the tradition of the elders? They don't wash their hands before they eat!" Jesus replied, "And why do you break the command of God for the sake of your tradition? For God said, 'Honor your father and mother' and 'Anyone who curses his father or mother must be put to death.' But you say that if a man says to his father or mother, 'Whatever help you might otherwise have received from me is a gift devoted to God,' he is not to 'honor his father' with it. Thus you nullify the word of God for the sake of your tradition. You hypocrites! Isaiah was right when he prophesied about you: 'These people honor me with their lips, but their hearts are far from me. They worship me in vain; their teachings are but rules taught by men.' "

Jesus called the crowd to him and said, "Listen and understand. What goes into a man's mouth does not make him 'unclean,' but what comes out of his mouth, that is what makes him 'unclean.' " Then the disciples came to him and asked, "Do you know that the Pharisees were offended when they heard this?" He replied, "Every plant that my heavenly Father has not planted will be pulled up by the roots. Leave them; they are blind guides. If a blind man leads a blind man, both will fall into a pit." (Matthew 15:1-14)

Someone Changed the Bulletin—Run!

It seemed like such an innocent decision at the time.

I had no idea that a bulletin could split a church.

In 1990, I was the associate pastor of a church in Vincennes, Indiana. The city of Vincennes, which sits on the Illinois state line, is a beautiful and tranquil city. The church had called me to minister to the youth, and I was about six weeks into my new position when the senior pastor abruptly resigned. I was faced with a hurting and confused congregation.

The problem was, I was a young and impetuous man in my early twenties, hardly old or mature enough to steer them through rough waters. Still, they were patient with me, and over the next year I served as the interim pastor. Amazingly, the church began to grow, though I was feeding them a steady diet of horrible sermons and insufficient pastoral skills.

As the church grew, the various ministries of the church became very busy. College ministries, discipleship teams, cell groups, and the like were all very successful. Each week, the bulletin overflowed with information and announcements. Perhaps due to my youthful ignorance, I never understood why we printed the entire service outline in the bulletin. Furthermore, it seemed insulting to me that we would then *read* the bulletin to the people during the time of announcements. These were highly educated people, and I felt we were treating them as if they were illiterate by reciting it to them. Could they not read for themselves?

So one otherwise uneventful week, I made an ill-advised and fateful decision. I decided that we would no longer print the service order in the bulletin. At the time I thought it was quite a spiritual epiphany because then we could leave space for the Holy Spirit to redirect the worship as needed. Though the order of our worship did not change in any substantial way, we simply did not print the order in the weekly handout.

The only change we made to the service was that we used the bulletin to highlight the many events taking place that week but did not waste any time reading it to the people. We made an announcement at the beginning and end of the service that the bulletin offered them numerous opportunities to serve God that week, and they should take time to see for themselves.

That first Sunday with the new weekly bulletin ran more smoothly than I could have imagined. The singing was more spontaneous, and the service seemed to flow better. The vast majority of the people in the congregation caught on quickly. I thought it was a rousing success.

Until Monday morning.

On Monday morning I arrived at the office to discover that a number of leaders had met secretly on Sunday night and were formulating a plan to confront me. They were furious with me and had approached several church leaders about this horrible development. My major infraction?

You guessed it—changing the bulletin.

How could something as banal and pallid as a bulletin almost split a church? Think about it for a minute: they had a special and secret meeting to discuss the offense of a change in the bulletin. Then they had a special meeting with me to air their grievances about a change in the bulletin. Then we had a church board meeting to attempt to reconcile those who had been offended by a change in the church bulletin.

In total, we must have spent forty hours rectifying the offense of a change in the church bulletin.

As I look back, I know now that I was attempting too great a change in an established congregation. I know now that many people see church as a bastion of the familiar, and in a hectic and frenzied world, they receive great comfort in knowing that the church will run as it always has run.

But is that real Christianity? Is that actually the way that Jesus designed the church? Before you begin reading this chapter, be forewarned. You may become offended by what you are about to read. I do not mean to be offensive, but you have to remember, I have no allegiance to traditions. I did not become a Christian until I was almost in college, so many of the tried-and-true recipes of Christian styles do not hold the same resonance to me as they may to you.

However, you may also be offended by the words of Jesus in this chapter. When confronted by the Pharisees over a minute detail of ablution, he called the most religious people of that day "hypocrites." He was much less gentle with traditions than most of us.

The Traditions of the Elders (Matthew 15:1-2)

Matthew 14 records many of our Lord's most famous miracles. Near Magdala on the shores of the Sea of Galilee he had fed thousands of people with the loaves and the fish. The number of the men was five thousand (Matthew 14:21), so adding in the women and the children, this number could well have been closer to ten thousand. Then he walked on the water and invited Peter to join him (Matthew 14:22-33). Finally, he healed many sick people in the city of Gennesaret, some who were healed simply by touching his robe (Matthew 14:34-36).

While he was in Gennesaret, some scribes and Pharisees approached him with a question designed to trap him. The text notes that they had traveled all the way from Jerusalem to this city on the northwestern shore of the Sea of Galilee for the sole purpose of asking him a question.

Why do your disciples not wash their hands in the proper manner as prescribed by our elders?

It seemed to be an odd and insignificant question, but much like the issue of the bulletin, it was fraught with meaning. In Mark's account the details are somewhat more telling:

> Now when they saw some of His disciples eat bread with defiled, that is, with unwashed hands, they found fault. For the Pharisees and all the Jews do not eat unless they wash their hands in a special way, holding the tradition of the elders. When they come from the marketplace, they do not eat unless they wash. And there are many other things which they have received and hold, like the washing of cups, pitchers, copper vessels, and couches. (Mark 7:2-4 NKJV)

The Jewish leaders had in years past developed many traditions that dictated the most devout manner to live as faithful Jews. These traditions were based on commentaries on the Old Testament laws and were called *Mishnah*. Scribes spent their lives developing entire doctrines based on these teachings, and the Pharisees held to these traditions in the strictest fashion.

The only problem with these traditions was that they were not scriptural. They were practices that had developed over time and become part of everyday Jewish life. Though they were based on the Law, they were not in the Law, and this difference was a profundity lost on them. To the scribes and the Pharisees, the traditions of the elders were equal to the commandments of God.

Corban, Your Father Is Calling (Matthew 15:3-6)

To Jesus, these traditions were self-contradictory. Some of the very traditions these leaders had established to follow the commandments of God actually had the opposite effect: they caused people to sin. Jesus immediately responded with an example of a Jewish tradition that broke the commandments of God.

The Pharisees had established a system by which an angry child could disavow his parents. Once he reached an adult age, if the child did not want to take care of his parents, he could declare that all his material possessions were devoted to God. The money that he would normally spend taking care of his elderly parents would instead go to the temple treasury. This practice was called *corban*.

Jesus cited the use of *corban* as a direct contradiction to the commandment to honor your father and mother (Exodus 20:12). In fact, the Pharisees had developed this practice so well that if the child later regretted his action, the Pharisees ruled that would be breaking a vow as cited in Numbers 30:2. Thus, once the money was declared, it could not be returned. Jesus said this nullified the very Law given by God.

You Are Nothing but a Fraud (Matthew 15:7-9)

It was a damning indictment, but Jesus was not finished yet. He called them "hypocrites," which comes from the Greek word *hypokrites*. The word describes an actor, playing a part behind a mask of pretense. The actor only pretends to be angry or happy, even though he may not actually be angry or happy. He is performing.

To further make his point, our Lord quoted Isaiah 29:13 and said, "These people honor me with their lips, but their hearts are far from me. They worship me in vain; their teachings are but rules taught by men." The denunciation was fervent, as the language of the text indicates Jesus' indignation at their attempt to trap him.

The second half of Jesus' condemnation is especially pertinent to our discussion of toxic faith. Seven hundred years before our Lord's birth, the prophet Isaiah recorded a censure of the development of doctrines made by mere people.

The Definition of Traditionalism

Jesus did not condemn consistency with the Law, but he placed a strong curse on human interpretation that twisted God's Word. One of the greatest moments of clarity in the life of a Christian comes when he or she is able to distinguish between human rules and God's truth. In fact, every single church in Christendom struggles with this very issue every single service. It is the issue of the aforementioned bulletin.

It is important to distinguish between tradition and traditionalism. Dr. C. Richard Wells made this abundantly clear in his presidential address at the Criswell College in the spring of 2002:

> I believe in traditions. Traditions are principles of Scripture that have been passed down over the generations. They are part of the living faith of dead men. But I despise traditionalism. Traditionalism is the exact opposite of tradition. If tradition is the living faith of dead men, then traditionalism is the dead faith of living men.

The difference cannot be stated strongly enough. A toxic faith is based on *traditionalism*. It says, "We have never done it that way before." It operates only in its comfort zone. It takes no chances, abides no change, and allows no deviance from the established order. The two terms are polar opposites.

> *Tradition is the living faith of the dead. Traditionalism is the dead faith of the living.*

The basis for tradition is *biblical principle*. For example, we are to pray when we come together, and pray without ceasing for one another (1 Thessalonians 5:17). This is a principle of the word of God. Churches that carry out the mandate given by God are commanded to pray without ceasing.

Traditionalism is based on *personal preference*. Allow me to give an example. In 2001 I presented a series of lectures on Islam in the Ukraine. On the Sunday after I lectured, I was invited to speak at a worship service in Zaporizhzhia. As with most churches in the region, there were no seats in the congregation. A few chairs were placed in the corners for older and disabled people, but otherwise the floor was empty.

Remarkably, the people stood for the entire service, and they did so every single week. They felt it was disrespectful to sit in the presence of God, and so they stood. When they began to pray, virtually all of the people raised their hands in the air and prayed simultaneously. Each person voiced a prayer, and the room sounded like it was filled with buzzing bees. For a man not accustomed to this type of prayer, it was disconcerting, yet glorious.

I had never seen anyone pray in this manner before. I had always been in churches where one person voiced the prayer publicly while everyone else prayed silently. When they took the Lord's Supper, they used a common cup. The deacons took the silver mug and placed it to the lips of each person standing in line and then wiped it with a white cloth. This practice was a bit more disturbing to me, especially since I have issues with germs!

Now imagine if, when I stood to preach that morning, I rebuked them for the way they prayed and took Communion. What if I told them that the manner in which they were worshiping was out of order and breaking the traditions as I understood them? Would that not be considered both rude and offensive?

Offering prayer during the worship service and taking Communion are issues of principle. They are firmly stated in Scripture and have ample tradition in the body of Christ.

The method of my prayer and my method of taking Communion are issues of preference. Certainly, I might feel more comfortable when the people pray in a manner with which I am familiar, but it would be sheer arrogance to state emphatically that my method is the only method to carry out that principle. Wouldn't you agree?

Warning: You Are about to Be Offended!

If we were to view all of our familiar worship and religious practices through the grid that Christ established in the issue of washing hands and *corban*, many of our worst church fights would seem silly. In the last twenty-five years of ministry, I have seen churches split over the use of choir robes, the color of the carpet, and the style of the pastor's hair. Truthfully, I am embarrassed when I think about how we Christians have bickered over the pettiest issues of preference and have offended a lost world.

On a weekly basis, as I travel and meet unbelievers, I am shocked by how many were rebuffed in their search for Christ by feuding churches, trivial issues, and insignificant preferences. In one instance, I saw a church vote out a pastor because he did not recognize the nursery workers during a banquet.

Now, are you ready to handle difficult truth? Just as Jesus distinguished between the teachings of people (traditionalism and preference) and the doctrines of God (tradition and principle), we should make the same allowance. Consider the worship service in your church last Sunday and ask yourself the following question: *is that an issue of preference or principle?* If it is an issue of preference, it is not worth getting upset over a change. If it is a matter of principle, it is worth defending. Look at the following chart, and please do not take offense.

Issue	Principle	Preference
Weekly service?	The disciples met regularly to worship.	Meeting at 11:00 a.m. *is a matter of preference.*
Meeting place?	The disciples gathered in various locations, including homes.	Meeting in a building called the church *is a matter of preference.*
Morning and evening services?	The disciples met daily in worship (Acts 5:42).	Having two services every Sunday *is a matter of preference.*
Use of a bulletin?	Not in Scripture.	Using a bulletin is a *preference.*
Announcements?	Not in Scripture.	Making announcements is a *preference.*
Use of instruments?	Many cited in worship in the Psalms (Psalm 150).	Using an organ and a piano versus a band *is a preference.*
Corporate singing?	Often invoked in the Bible, including Colossians 3:16	Singing three songs before the offering *is a preference.*

Special music?	Not mandated in Scripture.	The use of praise teams, soloists, and bands *is a matter of preference.*
Sermon style?	Sermons recorded in the New Testament were expository in nature (e.g., Stephen in Acts 7).	The use of humor, illustrations, alliteration, or a poem *is a preference.*
Sermon length?	Not stipulated. Paul preached so long that a young man fell asleep.	Sermon length *is a preference.*
Time to take the offering?	Not mandated. They took the offering every time they met.	Taking the offering before the sermon is *a preference.*
Communion?	"As often as you take" simply dictates a manner in which you take it (Matthew 26).	The number of times you take Communion *is a preference.*
People taking up the offering?	Not in Scripture.	Having only the deacons take the offering *is a preference.*
People serving Communion?	The deacons served the widows and orphans after the service (Acts 6).	Having only the deacons serve the Communion *is a preference.*
Service length?	Not stipulated in Scripture.	Ending at noon *is a preference.*
Dress code in church?	Not stipulated in Scripture.	Wearing a tie *is a matter of preference.*
Giving an invitation?	Each sermon in the New Testament was followed by a call to decision (Acts 3).	Singing four hundred verses of a slow song *is a matter of preference.*

Did reading the chart make your life difficult? If you are a normal Christian, it should have. Once I see the difference between that with which I am comfortable and that which is essential, I feel uncomfortable with my inconsequential objections during the worship. The essentials for genuine Christian fellowship are there, but my little protestations are insignificant in light of the mission of the church. Becoming a toxic believer is quite simple and subtle. All I have to do is allow my personal penchants to become a test of fellowship, and suddenly I am fighting over whether we have a clock on the back wall of the sanctuary.

One final example will make this even more difficult. In our current climate, many churches are fighting over the style of worship. Whether contemporary praise or traditional hymn style singing, churches quickly pick sides and defend their territory. Is this a matter of preference or principle? Certainly being able to understand the words of the songs is essential. Otherwise how can I praise God?

However, if we are genuinely seeking God's favor, could we not admit that certain styles may be understandable to some, even if they are not understandable to others? When I first became a Christian, I struggled with the songs in the hymnal. I did not understand many of the older English words, and the southern accent of many singers further confused me. I was a child educated in the Midwest during the 1970s and the 1980s, and the more progressive style of music was my language. *To this day* I struggle with styles such as gospel and bluegrass, and I am completely lost when someone sings in German.

When I mention this to some of my older ministerial friends, they quickly state that I could learn to love it if I really tried to love it. When I use the same argument to get them to listen to more contemporary styles of worship, they shrug off my suggestion as if I was asking them to break-dance. The irony is not lost on me.

Toxic believers vehemently defend their traditions as principle, not preference. They become either melancholy for the past or angry at the advent of new forms. They are comfortable only with that with which they are comfortable. To them, their traditionalism is good enough for everyone, and even questioning it is equivalent to heresy.

Tragically, the people who need to make this distinction most will never read this chapter. They stopped after the opening illustration because they too would have asked for my resignation. As Jesus stated at the end of the text, they are blind—and happily so. As the disciples noted in Matthew 15:12, they are offended at the mere mention of their traditions in a negative manner. In this instance, the poison causes blindness.

CHAPTER SEVEN
Church of the Frozen Smile

The Pharisees and Sadducees came to Jesus and tested him by ask-
ing him to show them a sign from heaven. He replied, "When
evening comes, you say, 'It will be fair weather, for the sky is red,'
and in the morning, 'Today it will be stormy, for the sky is red and
overcast.' You know how to interpret the appearance of the sky, but
you cannot interpret the signs of the times. A wicked and adulter-
ous generation looks for a miraculous sign, but none will be given
it except the sign of Jonah." Jesus then left them and went away.

When they went across the lake, the disciples forgot to take bread.
"Be careful," Jesus said to them. "Be on your guard against the
yeast of the Pharisees and Sadducees." They discussed this among
themselves and said, "It is because we didn't bring any bread."

Aware of their discussion, Jesus asked, "You of little faith,
why are you talking among yourselves about having no bread?
Do you still not understand? Don't you remember the five
loaves for the five thousand, and how many basketfuls you gath-
ered? Or the seven loaves for the four thousand, and how many
basketfuls you gathered? How is it you don't understand that I
was not talking to you about bread? But be on your guard
against the yeast of the Pharisees and Sadducees." Then they
understood that he was not telling them to guard against the
yeast used in bread, but against the teaching of the Pharisees and
Sadducees. (Matthew 16:1-12)

Keeping Up Appearances

The truth of the thesis of this chapter came to me *after* I was
married.

I am absolutely sure I am not alone in this admission, and given
the number of married Christians who are reading this book, I am
confident that you will agree as well. The worst fights my wife and
I have ever had . . . have been fought on the way to church.

Isn't that just like the devil? On a Sunday morning, you are driving in the car on your way to church, arguing about being late, and you are passing people getting into boats who look *much happier* than you do!

Jill and I had been married for a few years when we were pastoring in Colorado. One particular Sunday, we had to drive to church and were running late. Now, granted, we are usually late, but this particular Sunday we were later than usual. The problem was, as pastor, I had the job of ensuring that the church was unlocked. In our modern Christian culture, it is popular for pastors to hyphenate their title, such as pastor-teacher.

> *The worst fights my wife and I have ever had . . . have been fought* **on the way to church.**

Well, in the small church, the pastor is also hyphenated, except the title is not official. I was pastor-janitor, pastor-lawn care, and sometimes pastor-child care.

I had to get to the church in time to turn on the air-conditioning. We were *really* late.

As we drove, Jill and I were bickering about who had caused us to be late. She was explaining to me (quite forcefully) that dressing a baby is quite difficult, and if I had helped, perhaps we would not have been in this predicament. We were not arguing; we were fighting.

As the quarrel was moving toward an epiphany, we were pulling into the church parking lot. People were already there, milling about. What did we do? We did what every Christian couple in our situation would do.

We put on fake smiles, got out of the car, shook hands, and said "amen" and "good morning" many times. Sad, isn't it? Yet many Christians do this every given Sunday.

How do we get like this? How is it possible that believers in Jesus Christ, who understand that Christ's love and salvation fill us with joy, can become so bitter and angry? Listen to the accusations against Christians offered by nonbelievers:

Fake.

Fraudulent.

Plastic.

Counterfeit.

Phony.

Perhaps if we were honest, we would shamefacedly admit that this is truer than we would wish it were. Sometimes we are downright toxic.

How Did We Get Here? A Cynic's Journey

Can you remember back to the early days of your faith? Remember those first steps as a new believer, when you had the innocent faith to move mountains? You honestly knew that God could do anything. Your confidence in God was refreshing to your soul. Prayer was active and vital. Church was exciting. You *expected* God to do miracles, even in the little things. You knew God was capable.

Fast-forward a few years, and look in the mirror. It is often not pretty. We become hardened, caustic, and cynical. Churchgoing is no longer exciting but an exercise in boredom. Prayer (if it exists at all) is requisite and almost robotic. There is no *life* in our eternal life. Occasionally, we see God work in other people's lives, but we no longer expect God to do it *to us*. Where our vital and vibrant faith once was, there is a gaping chasm. We are believers, but we have settled for a stagnant form of faith. Like lifelong workers in a government job, we know what is expected of us, we know the limits of the job, and we know when quitting time comes.

The chasm is not empty. Since our souls abhor a vacuum, we become filled with a stoic and stony demeanor. We become filled with a simmering resentment against those who remind us of our bygone days of joy. We become cutting and biting, even during the time of prayer requests. When the Bible study opens up for questions, we ask the skeptic's questions, almost challenging the others in the class to dare to answer.

Welcome to the world of toxic faith. Like the Pharisees before us, we believe nothing, trust no one, and are obsessively suspicious.

Show Us That You Are from God (Matthew 16:1)

Does the question by the Pharisees sound familiar? It is the exact question with which they challenged Jesus before. In two chapters of Matthew, they confronted Jesus by demanding: *Prove* that you are sent from God. Show us that God has authenticated your ministry.

In both disputes, the Pharisees used the same Greek word—*semeion*. The term is explicit. It translates into a term that conveys absolute proof of validity. When a police officer stops you and walks up to your car, he or she asks for your driver's license and proof of insurance. The officer is asking for a sign, a *semeion*. The officer wants *proof* that you are who you say you are and that you have insurance.

Read Matthew 12:38 (NKJV): "Then some of the scribes and Pharisees answered, saying, 'Teacher, we want to see a sign from You.'" By calling him "Teacher," they were not necessarily giving him any respect. The word (*didaskalos*) does not always convey the respect that one would show to a rabbi. They were simply acknowledging that he was known as a teacher with some influence.

In the text for this chapter, the challenge was more pointed. The Pharisees asked for a "sign *from heaven*." They asked for unequivocal substantiation that Jesus was from God. Unlike the earlier request, here they were questioning his nature, not just his ability. In Matthew 12, they wanted to see if he was capable of performing a miracle. In Matthew 16, they demanded proof that he was who he said he was.

A comparison of various modern translations of Matthew 16:1 illuminates exactly how tense this confrontation was:

> Some Pharisees and Sadducees were on him again, pressing him to prove himself to them. (*The Message*)

> The Pharisees and Sadducees came to Jesus, wanting to trick him. So they asked him to show them a miracle from God. (NCV)

> Some Pharisees and Sadducees who came to Jesus wanted to trap him, so they asked him to perform a miracle for them, to show that God approved of him. (GNT)

It was not a casual or offhanded request. It was an inquisition. The language of the Greek text expresses their preconceived disbelief. They approached Jesus as skeptics. They despised the fact that he had garnered a following, and their question was hostile and antagonistic. It was not a friendly challenge; it was a dare. They were skeptical and critical simultaneously.

You'll Get Over It, Honey

This type of cynicism and caustic faith does not develop suddenly. It slowly arises over the course of time. With every series of spiritual disappointments, the toxic person begins to settle into a sarcastic disposition.

Twenty-five years ago, I served as a youth pastor at a church in Kentucky. The church had never participated in a student mission trip, so there was considerable excitement as our group of fifteen youth left for Ohio to lead Bible clubs and evangelism in an impoverished section of an industrial town. The plan was to do one-on-one soul-winning at the clubs and to lead a student revival in the evenings.

When we returned home, the report we presented on Sunday night was electric. Most of the boys had never won anyone to Christ, so the experience had profoundly touched them. As one young man rose to the pulpit to share, he became choked with emotion when he recalled the joy of winning two brothers to faith in Jesus. He told of going to their home where they lived with their grandmother in the projects, and her weeping when her grandsons told her that they had become Christians. By the time he finished telling the story, virtually the entire congregation was smiling as well, with only a few dry eyes.

After the service, the members filed by the boys and hugged them and spoke briefly. Most communicated that they were so proud of these mountain kids becoming short-term missionaries. Many remarked that they thought it was one of the greatest worship services they had ever experienced.

With the exception of one woman.

One sweet stalwart of the congregation, Agnes, listened intently as the young man spoke of the joy he felt. When he talked about the boys, his eyes filled again with tears, and he exclaimed, "I wish this day would never end! I wish I were back there right now."

Agnes offered a faint half-smile, shook his hand, and coldly said, "Don't worry, honey. You'll get over it."

Enter the Pharisees.

When Christians, especially new ones, begin to realize the depths of God's love, they often become overwhelmed by the magnitude of God's grace and blessings. They have a pure and undiluted faith that anticipates God's great touch. Toxic believers, however, can douse any spiritual fire with a barbed word or phrase that immediately punctures the proceedings. Their genetic disposition toward hardened disbelief disguised as realism contaminates everything around them.

You Can't Handle the Truth (Matthew 16:2-5)

Jesus' response to the confrontation by the Pharisees was classic. Often in Scripture, our Lord would turn an argument against his accusers. Though the religious leaders asked for a sign (*semeion*), Jesus said that even if he *would* show them a sign, they *could not* understand it. He used the exact word that they used.

His illustration was meteorological. The Pharisees could read and interpret the skies and the weather changes, but they could not discern the truth of a sign if it was apparent to everyone else around them. They were not ready for the truth because they would not accept it. For truth to be believed, it must first be received.

A perfect illustration of this premise is the lifelong pessimist in your church. Regardless of the service and regardless of the blessing, the cynical and poisonous person can find the dark cloud. If the service goes too long because so many people are dealing with God, this person complains that the light bill will be expensive. If the church has to add another service because of growth, this person complains because of the wear and tear on the furniture.

A peculiar minister served on my ordination council. Based on stories I've heard from other ministers, it seems that every ordination council has at least *one* minister who infects the entire proceeding. This particular man had served in a series of churches where he apparently did not see God move as he wished. He sat in the corner of the room, brooding, as the other ministers peppered me with doctrinal questions. For anyone who has been a part of an ordination, you can predict the line of investigation:

- What must a person do to be saved?
- What are your beliefs on Christ's return?
- What did Jesus mean when he referred to the kingdom?
- Define and describe the Trinity.

I had studied intensely for months and felt prepared for whatever theological minutiae would arise. For approximately two hours, I sat still as these men played "stump the preacher boy." I enjoyed every single question, and given my proclivity for debate, I thoroughly took pleasure in the exchange.

Throughout the entire period, this gentleman remained quiet. He sat with his head bowed, as if he was listening to us discuss theological issues and hypothetical situations. As the drilling came to an end, the ministers asked me a series of "what would you do if . . ." questions. Since these questions were purely theoretical, I mustered my bravado and attempted to sound strong.

Suddenly, this gentleman spoke, and for the next twenty minutes, his questions became increasingly depressing:

- What would you do if your elders are godless and wicked?
- What would you do if your wife runs away with the choir leader?
- What do you do the day after you are fired by the church?
- What would you do if the church withholds your salary?

I was a twenty-one-year-old, wide-eyed young minister who expected to see a revival break out. My optimism clashed abruptly with his pessimism that bordered on psychosis. Every time I rejoined with a spiritual answer he became increasingly hostile. He interrupted me and almost disputed the possibility of my solution.

Thankfully, the other ministers were mortified at his line of questioning, and after he had blown off some steam, they attempted to quiet him down. Yet he was insistent that the ministry was a dark, gaping chasm of disappointment. In his mind, he was preparing me for ministry. In reality, he was making me spiritually suicidal.

Perhaps now you can understand the import of Jesus' response. When it comes to toxic believers, the premise is clear: it is not that pharisees are unable to understand the truths of Christian victory. Pharisees *do not want* to understand them. They are insulated by the safety of their cynicism.

The Infection of the Leaven (Matthew 16:6-12)

After he addressed the religious leaders, Jesus warned the disciples to "beware of the leaven of the Pharisees" (Matthew 16:6-7 NKJV). His statement to them was in direct response to their confrontation. However, the apostles missed the point. They assumed that Jesus was talking about their need for actual food. They, like the Pharisees, were letting their concern for physical security override spiritual realities, their faith and trust in God.

> *It is not that pharisees are unable to understand the truths of Christian victory. Pharisees* do not want *to* understand them. *They are insulated by the safety of their cynicism.*

Jesus heard their speculation and then responded to them. His instruction to them is also great coaching to us. Sometimes we are called to confront evil, but on occasion we are called to avoid it because of its deleterious effects on us personally.

Toxic faith invades a fellowship. One of the classic symptoms of toxic persons is that *their* drama becomes *your* drama. It overwhelms you and becomes the major issue. The Pharisees, pushing their way through the crowd just to ask their question, illustrated this point. People with this malady are uninterested unless they are center stage.

Toxic faith infects a fellowship. Eventually, the toxicity of these people becomes airborne. They change the tenor of every discussion because they insist on changing the direction of every discussion. Jesus warned against their growing effect.

Toxic faith influences a fellowship. Tragically, those who are most radically injured by these people are those who are not immune to their flawed reasoning and teachings. Like the older woman after the mission service, they assume a position of maturity and mock that which is wholesome and believing. If believers are not careful, these people gain an audience and an ever-increasing influence.

Jesus specifically called the disciples to avoid the teaching (*didache*) of the Pharisees. This is a reference to their power to manipulate other people, especially young believers.

A Final Word: Don't You Get It? God Is Still in Control

As Jesus sought to dissuade the disciples from the Pharisees' influence, he offered examples of his power and might. Referencing the feeding of the five thousand (John 6:1-14), he reminded them that he was able to show signs at will. Jesus was able to provide even more than what was expected or needed, as proved by the baskets of leftover bread (Matthew 16:9). He is never shorthanded and never has a shortfall.

> In a parallel story in the Gospels, Jesus went further and diagnosed the disease of the leaven. He said, "But woe to you Pharisees! For you tithe mint and rue and all manner of herbs, and pass by justice and the love of God. These you ought to have done, without leaving the others undone" (Luke 11:42 NKJV).

Their problem was not with Jesus' ability to produce a sign from heaven but their ability to actually believe in him. As Jesus noted, they were much better at following hollow rituals such as tithing on the smallest parts of their income, without understanding the "love of God." It was not a statement against tithing. The point is, tithing is the beginning of Christian stewardship, not the end. Giving anything—service, treasure, or a witness—without the proper heart is, in biblical terms, obedience without grace and mercy. It is ritual.

In Mark's account, Jesus' words to the apostles were marked by his frustration with the nature of signs. Though Jesus was (and is) capable of working wonders, our ability to be grateful and faithful is in direct correlation to our memory. Simply put, we forget his work yesterday when we face problems today. Thus, Jesus said, "Do you not yet perceive nor understand? Is your heart still hardened? Having eyes, do you not see? And having ears, do you not hear? And do you not remember?" (Mark 8:17-18 NKJV).

It is entirely possible that Jesus' frustration with the Pharisees' inability to believe was matched by his frustration with the apostles' inability to remember. A lack of gratitude is just as bad as a lack of faith.

CHAPTER EIGHT

Anyone Got Some Rocks?

*When Jesus had finished saying these things, he left Galilee and
went into the region of Judea to the other side of the Jordan.
Large crowds followed him, and he healed them there.*

*Some Pharisees came to him to test him. They asked, "Is it
lawful for a man to divorce his wife for any and every reason?"
"Haven't you read," he replied, "that at the beginning the
Creator 'made them male and female,' and said, 'For this reason a
man will leave his father and mother and be united to his wife,
and the two will become one flesh'? So they are no longer two,
but one. Therefore what God has joined together, let man not
separate." "Why then," they asked, "did Moses command that a
man give his wife a certificate of divorce and send her away?" Jesus
replied, "Moses permitted you to divorce your wives because your
hearts were hard. But it was not this way from the beginning.
I tell you that anyone who divorces his wife, except for marital
unfaithfulness, and marries another woman commits adultery."*

*The disciples said to him, "If this is the situation between a
husband and wife, it is better not to marry." Jesus replied, "Not
everyone can accept this word, but only those to whom it has
been given. For some are eunuchs because they were born that
way; others were made that way by men; and others have
renounced marriage because of the kingdom of heaven. The one
who can accept this should accept it." (Matthew 19:1-12)*

Rock Collectors

This story is especially tragic because it is true. I have changed
the names and some of the circumstances, however.

I did not hear the rumor until Wednesday night prayer meeting.

True, I had not seen either Kirk or Jessica in a number of weeks,
but I had assumed that they were on vacation. Summertime in the

South is often marked by family vacations to the beach, and the Smithfields had always taken advantage of their kids' break from school to follow suit. They had a small place on the beach and often left after they got off work on Friday, only to return late Sunday night.

The members of our small church entered the sanctuary whispering fervently, and as we began the service, I took prayer requests. Normally, I wrote these requests on a marker board and members wrote them short letters of encouragement, telling the people listed that they were praying for them.

On this particular Wednesday, one member stood and haltingly shared a prayer request that took me by surprise: "Please pray for Kirk and Jessica. They are getting a divorce. It is an ugly situation." She quickly sat down, and I just stood there for a second, unsure of what exactly I was going to do.

The Smithfields were not particularly faithful members of the church, but you could count on them to be sitting in the back a couple of times a month. Their children were active in the youth group, and Jessica had helped in a number of ministries through the years. A middle-class couple in their forties, Kirk and Jessica were attractive and fit people who worked full-time and successful jobs.

I made a visit to their home but found only Kirk. He was busy packing boxes in the garage and had little time for me. He gave no details, and quite frankly, I did not ask for any. I simply asked if everything was all right. He told me that he was moving out. He seemed uncomfortable with the discussion and quickly ended the conversation. He never used the word *divorce*, but he did say that I was not going to see either of them for a while.

Most disturbingly, he did not seem particularly emotional. They had been married more than fifteen years, yet he spoke of moving out as if he were discussing a football game in which he was casually interested. He never stopped working on his boxes the entire time we spoke. I could readily tell that I was a disturbance.

Over the course of weeks, details began to emerge. Apparently, Kirk and Jessica had caught each other in inappropriate relationships. Neither was invested in the extramarital affair, but both were resolute that the marriage was over. Though Kirk moved out, he stayed relatively close for the sake of the children.

As often is the case, people in the community took sides. Salacious details were whispered. Accusations were disclosed. It *did* become ugly. On those rare occasions when either of them came to church, the situation was awkward. Kirk or Jessica would come alone and sit alone in the back. Few in the church attempted to speak to either of them. It was as if they were being frozen out by our fellowship.

If someone *did* speak to one of them, that person was dragged into the drama. Christian gossip is often worse than non-Christian gossip because it is accompanied by prayer requests. As much as I tried to speak to both of them, the situation seemed hopeless. They were considered pariahs in our church. Eventually, they moved away and divorced.

I have not seen them or heard from them in years. Why are we so quick to pick up stones? Why do we treat the fallen as if they had leprosy?

There was never a public fight or a melee in the fellowship hall. No one formally stood up to bring spiritual charges against the couple. No one suggested church discipline.

No, what we did was far *worse*.

We turned them into outcasts.

We buried them alive. They had no one to whom they could turn, and no one who would offer objective advice. They must have felt alone and abandoned, and without any Christian encouragement.

Awkward Moments of Unfortunate Congratulations and Condolences

It was not as if no one tried. Our stumbling attempts at speaking to them, however, only made the situation worse. We did not know *what* to say. It is similar to when you go through a receiving line, either at a wedding or at a funeral. This is especially true when you do not know the people involved. Protocol demands that you offer a few words as you shake their hands, so you muster some feeble attempt at conversation.

In a wedding, the situation is relatively easier since it is a joyous occasion. You can shake the hands of the bride and groom and offer your congratulations. If you are distantly related to them, you can even give them a hug and a quick kiss on the cheek. Yet the conversation is still clumsy. Over the years I have been a part of so many weddings, I believe I have heard some of the most interesting things said at this moment. Second only to an inappropriate toast at the reception, these are some pithy statements to avoid:

- "Wow, you look skinnier than I expected."
- "But this isn't the guy I saw you with a few months ago."
- "Are your parents still fighting?"
- "I have a good lawyer. Here is his card."
- "If it doesn't work out, call me. I'm single."

A funeral is much more difficult when you do not know the deceased. You grieve with the widow or widower, and you sympathize with the person's pain, but again, it is awkward. You never really know which words are comforting and which ones are just uncomfortable. In more than two decades, I have heard some amazingly unfortunate comments:

- "Did he always wear a wig?"
- "Well, he can't hear you now, so he is at peace . . ."
- "He looks so natural with that makeup."
- "Heaven just got much louder . . ."

Perhaps the most ill-timed thing I have heard was a gentleman in line remarking that the deceased owed him money and asking the widow about it. Can you imagine? Still, you cannot judge the person speaking because we have all been in a similar position.

Public Spectacles of Private Problems

The sin we are discussing is not the faltering words of well-meaning saints who want to give comfort. The toxin that infects a fellowship comes from those who immediately attack the fallen. They make public spectacles of the private pains of others.

No other story in Scripture more clearly illustrates this problem than that of the woman caught in adultery (John 8). In a moving narrative, the Bible captures this particular situation:

> Jesus went to the Mount of Olives. And early in the morning He came again into the temple, and all the people were coming to

Him; and He sat down and began to teach them. And the scribes and the Pharisees brought a woman caught in adultery, and having set her in the midst, they said to Him, "Teacher, this woman has been caught in adultery, in the very act. Now in the Law Moses commanded us to stone such women; what then do You say?" And they were saying this, testing Him, in order that they might have grounds for accusing Him. But Jesus stooped down, and with His finger wrote on the ground. But when they persisted in asking Him, He straightened up, and said to them, "He who is without sin among you, let him be the first to throw a stone at her." And again He stooped down, and wrote on the ground. And when they heard it, they began to go out one by one, beginning with the older ones, and He was left alone, and the woman, where she had been, in the midst. And straightening up, Jesus said to her, "Woman, where are they? Did no one condemn you?" And she said, "No one, Lord." And Jesus said, "Neither do I condemn you; go your way. From now on sin no more." (vv. 1-11 NASB)

It was a problem with no seeming solution. This woman had clearly been caught in the act of adultery, and as the Pharisees and scribes brought her into the temple, they dragged her into the middle of the large court where people gathered to hear the teaching. According to the text, it was apparently an open-and-shut case (John 8:4, "in the very act").

The Pharisees and scribes even had the Law on their side. In Deuteronomy 22:22-27, Moses recorded God's provisions concerning those who were discovered to be having secret affairs and sexual relations outside of marriage.

In truth, the text was revolutionary because it protected the woman if she was raped. Early societies often blamed both parties or made the proof of rape so difficult that female victims were put to death beside their rapists. However, Deuteronomy 22:25-26 (NKJV) states, "If a man . . . forces her and lies with her, then only the man who lay with her shall die. But you shall do nothing to the young woman; there is in the young woman no sin worthy of death."

This was seemingly not the case here, however. This woman was not only complicit in the affair, but she had also been caught during the sexual act. Interestingly, the Pharisees and scribes did not deem it important to bring along the man with whom she was having relations.

The woman stood judged according to the biblical text: "If a man is found lying with a woman married to a husband, then both of them shall die. . . . You shall bring them both out to the gate of that city, and you shall stone them to death" (Deuteronomy 22:22-24 NKJV).

It seemed as if they had Jesus trapped. If Jesus did not call for her stoning, then he would be proclaimed to be a false teacher, going directly against the law of God. If he affirmed her stoning, then he would be viewed as cold and unsympathetic, and lose the popular support of the people.

In light of this dilemma, Jesus did an astonishing thing. John recorded that Jesus kneeled on the ground and silently began writing in the dirt with his finger. His silence must have infuriated the scribes and Pharisees because they "persisted in asking Him" what should be done (John 8:7 NASB).

Jesus rose and spoke one simple sentence. He said the person who had never sinned should be the first to throw a stone. Then he returned to the kneeling position and continued to write.

Many have speculated about what he was writing (John 8:8). Some conjecture that he was writing the names of the consorts of the Pharisees with whom they were having secret affairs. Others suggest that he was merely giving them time to consider his challenge. Perhaps he was just drawing a line in the sand over which they must step to begin stoning the woman.

Yet the silence was broken, not by rocks being thrown but by rocks being dropped. The Bible states, "They began to go out one by one" (John 8:9 NASB). The elders in their group were the first to retreat, followed by the younger Pharisees. Indeed, even casual observers of the drama were so taken aback by Jesus' words that they walked away, because the end of the passage records that soon just Jesus and the woman were left in the center of the temple courtyard.

While the crowd dispersed, Jesus had remained in the kneeling position, but now Jesus straightened up and asked the woman, "Is anyone left here to condemn you?"

She must have been relieved to respond, "No one, Lord." Then Jesus told her that he did not condemn her, either. I must hasten to say that Christ did not excuse her sin or give her free rein to do it again. He told her to "sin no more." But his purpose was restoration, not retribution.

Rescue the Perishing; Care for the Dying

Showing compassion, as expressed by that hymn we sing, is easy to do when the perishing are those who do not know Jesus. We excuse their sin because they do not know any other way. We pray for their salvation and extend grace to them. Christians are very good at being loving to the lost.

It is also relatively simple to be merciful to the dying because it is a journey we all must travel. Each and every day we walk toward death; and those who have been bowed by illness, disease, or age automatically have our empathy. We feel for them because one day, we shall *be* them.

It is *infinitely more* difficult to rescue those who are dying by their own hands. It is immensely more difficult to have mercy on those who should know better. Often the church responds with more vitriol on its own than on outsiders. To put it in common parlance, we eat our young.

Meet Mr. Schadenfreude

Why would the Pharisees joyfully approach Jesus with a situation as grim as a public stoning? Why would they gleefully drag a woman who was probably half-naked before Jesus in the local synagogue to present her before she was publicly killed? Reread verse 3 of John 8. They brought her into the very room where Jesus was teaching a large crowd and seated her right in the middle of the crowd. They made a public display of her and presented her as evidence. Why?

The answer is found in a German word, *schadenfreude*. The word is a compound of two smaller words, *schaden*, which means "pain" or "damage," and *freude*, which means "joy" or "delight." They took great pleasure in the pain of others. The woman was inconsequential to the Pharisees and scribes; she was simply a tool. They used her for their own purposes.

This toxin infects a fellowship and comes from those who rejoice at other people's suffering. They delight in the stories of other people's sins. Certainly, you know others who secretly rejoice when other people fall. What would cause such an ungodly response? It

> *Toxic Christians rejoice when others fall because it makes their job easier. They do not have to work to be more holy; they just have to compare themselves to someone else.*

is another central premise of toxic faith: toxic Christians rejoice when others fall because it makes their job easier. They do no have to work to be more holy; they just have to compare themselves to someone else.

These types of people view Christianity as a competition. Tragically, they feel better when you feel worse. Rather than help a fallen brother or sister, they pause for a minute and let their mental scorecard calculate. Rather than pursue God in holiness, they watch the fallen and secretly rejoice.

The Bible speaks of people who sadistically enjoy other people's pain, though the verses often go unnoticed:

Whoever gloats over disaster will not go unpunished.
(Proverbs 17:5)

Do not rejoice when your enemy falls,
And do not let your heart be glad when he stumbles. (Proverbs 24:17 NKJV)

Do not gloat over your brother's day,
The day of his misfortune.
And do not rejoice over the sons of Judah
In the day of their destruction;
Yes, do not boast
In the day of their distress. (Obadiah 12 NASB)

The interesting part of this advice is that such perverse happiness is usually displayed only by the enemies of God. Do you remember the words of David in Psalm 35:15? He wrote,

At my stumbling they rejoiced and gathered themselves together;
The smiters whom I did not know gathered together against me,
They slandered me without ceasing. (NASB)

Perhaps no biblical character felt the sting of brotherly attack as much as Job. As his world fell apart, his four "comforters" sat by his side and blamed him. Yet rather than respond with the same convoluted emotions, Job remarked that he had not "rejoiced at the extinction of [his] enemy, or exulted when evil befell him" (Job 31:29 NASB). In fact in the next verse, Job went as far as to call this type of action a sin.

So, What about the Divorce Question?

It seems strange that we would begin a chapter with a text referencing divorce and then move to another trap set by the Pharisees on the topic of stoning, does it not? Yet in both instances, the issue was the same. In both cases and in both questions, the Pharisees were making a public spectacle over a private pain. In both cases, they were looking for loopholes for themselves and yet stricture for anyone else.

During Jesus' time, there were two prevailing schools of thought in the Jewish world concerning divorce. Those who had been trained in the school of Shammai were very strict; they believed divorce should be allowed only in stringent circumstances. Other Jewish teachers followed a man named Hillel, who allowed for divorce in many instances. It could be that the Hillel followers approached Jesus because the question they asked in Matthew 19:3 is so vague ("Is it lawful for a man to divorce his wife for *any and every* reason?" [emphasis added]).

Jesus' answer seems to line up with the conservative school. He allowed divorce only in cases of infidelity (19:9). The surprising detail (often missed), however, is in Jesus' rationale for his answer. God brings couples together (v. 5), but the hardness of human hearts tears them apart (v. 8). The universal struggle of humans— the difficulty of life, the complexity of personalities, and the sheer weight of existence—would cause all relationships to crumble!

Do you understand more completely now why the disciples responded as they did in 19:10 ("It is better not to marry")? Who can possibly make any relationship work?

Jesus did not just go back to the Law of Moses to illustrate the point. He used an interesting phrase in Matthew 19:8 (NKJV): "from the beginning it was not so." It is a direct reference to the original battling spouses—Adam and Eve.

The Original Dysfunctional Family: Adam and Eve

When caught defying God's instructions, Adam and Eve reflexively responded by blaming each other. They were united in sin and divided from God. If any couple should have thrown in the towel, it should have been Adam and Eve. In short order, they blamed each other before God, lost their home, were forced to eke out a meager existence outside the garden of Eden, raised three sons—one a victim, one a homicidal maniac, one who "made it"—and generally lived in chaos.

Yet Jesus quoted from their wedding vows, written by God the Father: "So they are no longer two, but one. Therefore what God has joined together, let man not separate" (19:6). Their marriage was difficult because *life is difficult*. The collision of the two stories of this chapter—the woman caught in adultery and the question on divorce—came from shortsighted people.

In John 8, perhaps Jesus was writing down the names of the women with whom the Pharisees and scribes were having affairs. Perhaps he was listing the many sins committed by all the people in the crowd. Perhaps he was just giving them time to consider their sins. In any case, the realization dawned on the crowd: *we all deserve stoning*, and *we all need mercy*.

Knowing the exhausting nature of marriage, life, families, jobs, and children, we should perhaps ask, "How can any marriage stay together?" It seems impossible. The only answer is God as the common foundation.

Only God could bring together two people and keep them together. Only God could forgive a woman caught in the act of sexual sin. Only God could keep Job from suicide when his world was destroyed. Only God could keep Hosea married to a woman as unfaithful as Gomer.

When we feel that we have every reason to run from our relationships, Jesus reminds us that God united us for a purpose. When we feel that the situation is hopeless, he reminds us that others have had it worse and survived. When we see nothing but a bleak future, Jesus reminds us of his faithfulness in our past.

Jesus' point was not to define the permissions and parameters of relationships, but to reiterate the foundation for healthy ones. Only God can rescue us from ourselves. Only God can keep us from becoming pharisees. Forgiveness makes a merciful heart.

The only real, lasting cure for toxic Christians is experiencing the love of God in a deeper way.

CHAPTER NINE
When Jesus Lays the Smack Down

Responding to Toxic Faith

[Jesus said,] "Woe to you, teachers of the law and Pharisees, you hypocrites! You shut the kingdom of heaven in men's faces. You yourselves do not enter, nor will you let those enter who are trying to.

"Woe to you, teachers of the law and Pharisees, you hypocrites! You travel over land and sea to win a single convert, and when he becomes one, you make him twice as much a son of hell as you are.

"Woe to you, blind guides! You say, 'If anyone swears by the temple, it means nothing; but if anyone swears by the gold of the temple, he is bound by his oath.' You blind fools! Which is greater: the gold, or the temple that makes the gold sacred? You also say, 'If anyone swears by the altar, it means nothing; but if anyone swears by the gift on it, he is bound by his oath.' You blind men! Which is greater: the gift, or the altar that makes the gift sacred? Therefore, he who swears by the altar swears by it and by everything on it. And he who swears by the temple swears by it and by the one who dwells in it. And he who swears by heaven swears by God's throne and by the one who sits on it.

"Woe to you, teachers of the law and Pharisees, you hypocrites! You give a tenth of your spices—mint, dill, and cummin. But you have neglected the more important matters of the law—justice, mercy and faithfulness. You should have practiced the latter, without neglecting the former. You blind guides! You strain out a gnat but swallow a camel.

"Woe to you, teachers of the law and Pharisees, you hypocrites! You clean the outside of the cup and dish, but inside they are full of greed and self-indulgence. Blind Pharisee! First clean the inside of the cup and dish, and then the outside also will be clean.

"Woe to you, teachers of the law and Pharisees, you hypocrites! You are like whitewashed tombs, which look beautiful on

the outside but on the inside are full of dead men's bones and everything unclean. In the same way, on the outside you appear to people as righteous but on the inside you are full of hypocrisy and wickedness.

"*Woe to you, teachers of the law and Pharisees, you hypocrites! You build tombs for the prophets and decorate the graves of the righteous. And you say, 'If we had lived in the days of our forefathers, we would not have taken part with them in shedding the blood of the prophets.' So you testify against yourselves that you are the descendants of those who murdered the prophets. Fill up, then, the measure of the sin of your forefathers!*

"*You snakes! You brood of vipers! How will you escape being condemned to hell?" (Matthew 23:13-33)*

Pain and Torture in Thailand

No, the section heading is not a story about a political prisoner in some dark dungeon. It is far worse.

It concerns a massage I received in Bangkok, Thailand.

In March 2008, I was invited to teach at a Bible institute in Thailand, a beautiful and exotic place. The verdant landscape is offset by the bustling city, teeming with millions of people. I taught students throughout the course of a week on the doctrines of Islam and had an amazing time. They were receptive, gracious, and very attentive. Standing on my feet for hours on end was quite tiresome; and by the end of the week, I was as drained as I had ever felt. The worst pain was in my back, where I honestly felt there were little men banging away on my spine with tiny hammers.

As I mentioned this to the chancellor of the institute, he said something in Thai and smiled. Not knowing the language, I defaulted to my automatic response when I am on a mission field without language skills: I smiled and nodded in agreement. He rushed off and made a phone call as I completed my teaching assignment that afternoon.

Following the class, a large number of men from the institute, including me, piled into a series of cars, and we traveled slowly through the city. Bangkok during rush hour looks remarkably like a parking lot after a football game. The lines in the street were mere suggestions with small bicycles weaving through the cars as if they were abandoned.

After an hour, we arrived at a building no bigger than a convenience store. As we entered the building, beautiful instrumental music played over a sound system, and a fountain trickled a stream of water through the lobby. I removed my shoes and sat on a cushiony sofa. I was handed a pungent tea to drink.

We sat for a few moments until a hostess entered the lobby. She was a short woman with a friendly manner, and she motioned to us to enter the back of the building. We walked through hanging bamboo curtains, into a large dressing room, where we were told to remove our outer clothes. Since she did not speak English, I assume that is what she said. Actually, I will never know what she said, but I wasn't about to remove my undergarments! Thankfully, none of the other men did, either. I was afraid this was going to turn into some made-for-television movie, but since the men traveling with me were pastors, I felt somewhat safer.

We put on large robes and slippers and were ushered into another, larger room. The room, which smelled like fresh flowers and incense, was lined with long cushions on the floor, covered in towels. Each man took a cushion and sat down, so I followed suit. They spoke to one another in Thai and upon occasion spoke to me in broken English. Apparently, it was a therapeutic salon. At least that is what I hoped it was. The instrumental music played in the darkened room, and I almost fell asleep.

After a few minutes, a number of very short, diminutive women entered the room. Not one of them was over five feet tall or under eighty years old in my estimation. I began to wonder, *How is this little woman* ever *going to be able to work the kinks out of my back?* I stand six feet tall and weigh a metric ton. Okay, perhaps the weight is a bit of an exaggeration, but not by much. The point is, I was three times the size of the kind-looking woman who stood before me and shook my hand.

I joked to one of the men that I could twirl this woman like a baton. How could she ever give me a massage?

It was the last time I joked or laughed that day. In the span of about one hour, this tiny little woman proceeded to mangle me into shapes that I have never taken. Her hands must have been made of granite; and she was obviously a power lifter in her spare time because she reduced me to a blubbering mass in seconds.

A Thai massage is not so much a chiropractic realignment as it is a method of anguish and suffering. If the Roman Catholics had used this during the Inquisition, every single Reformer would have recanted. Each single movement was more painful than the last. She stood behind me and planted her knees in my back and twisted my shoulders. At one point, I believe I was able to touch the small of my back with my nose, but that is unconfirmed. At least it felt like I could.

She never spoke and never smiled. In fact, I don't think she ever even breathed. The woman was able to turn me into a jellyroll of mangled limbs. She quickly moved from my upper back to my lower back, where she apparently removed my spine, set it on the side table, and twisted every muscle. I have never felt such pain in all of my life. I would rather have a root canal without medication than to experience that again.

What made the experience even more humiliating was that, after the massage, I had to stand to my feet and *thank her,* as all the other men were doing. This woman beat me like I owed her money, and I had to thank her. I believe at one point I began to cry. I am not sure of that because I believe I had passed out from the pain at the time. My only indication that I had wept was the fact that the other men in the room kept pointing at me and saying, "Little girl."

The indignity of thanking my torturer! Having to actually be grateful for my anguish at the hands of this octogenarian sadist! I was able to manage only a feeble *thank you* as I stumbled into the daylight after our experience. I still have not found my spine.

Can you imagine the dignity of our Lord in the face of his accusers? Throughout his earthly ministry, the Pharisees had hounded him, mocked him, and accused him of every malfeasance under the Law. They continually attempted to indict him of trumped-up charges, and trick him into committing treason against the Roman state.

All the while, Jesus patiently answered their questions and rebuffed their attacks. Knowing that the crowd was watching every exchange, Jesus showed remarkable patience in the face of raw vile. Those men did not deserve such graciousness, but Jesus extended it anyway.

Let the Verbal Beatings Commence (Matthew 21)

For more than three years, the religious leaders attacked our Lord. Then Jesus entered the last week of his earthly life as recorded in Matthew 21. As Christ triumphantly entered the city of Jerusalem riding on a donkey, the people lined the city streets, waving palm branches and singing, "Hosanna to the Son of David! / Blessed is He who comes in the name of the LORD! / Hosanna in the highest!" (Matthew 21:1-9 NKJV). It must have been an amazing sight because Matthew recorded that "all the city was moved" (21:10 NKJV). The people were openly proclaiming that Jesus was the Messiah and the "Son of David." The city reverberated with the declaration.

In response, the Pharisees increased the ferocity of their attacks. Jesus was a real and present danger to their power. He was a threat to their very existence! If he *was* the "Son of David," he would establish and take his rightful place on the throne. In short, they would be out of a job.

Over the course of the next three days, the Pharisees verbally attacked Jesus at every turn. He was on their turf in Jerusalem, and they viewed him as an interloper. He was a danger, and they were going to see to it that he was stopped. Take some time and review the battles in those early days after his entrance into the Holy City.

Jesus threw the money changers out of the temple (Matthew 21:12-17). While the charlatans were making a great amount of money inside the temple courts, the religious leaders were furious at Jesus. When the chief priests and scribes heard the children calling Jesus the "Son of David," they were "indignant" (Matthew 21:15 NKJV). The Greek word for their anger in that verse is *aganakteo*, which is the strongest form of the term. It means they were "filled with uncontrollable fury."

Using a parable about a landlord, Jesus directly confronted the religious leaders (Matthew 21:33-46). He told the crowd a story of a man who built a vineyard and then leased it to some workers. With the approach of the harvest season, he sent three servants to collect the rent, but when they came into the fields, the tenants killed one servant, stoned another, and beat the third one. The landowner sent another group of servants, but they were treated viciously. Finally, the landowner sent his son, assuming that the tenants would respect the son of the landowner more. Instead, the tenants decided that they would kill the son and take over the vineyard.

When Jesus asked the crowd what the landowner should do, the crowd responded that he should "bring those wretches to a wretched end" (Matthew 21:41). The chief priests and the Pharisees, who were in the crowd, knew he was talking about them. They were the ungrateful tenants, who had rejected the prophets who came before them, and then ultimately they attacked the Son of God, who was the ultimate landowner. The chapter ends ominously with these words, "When the chief priests and the Pharisees heard Jesus' parables, they knew he was talking about them. They looked for a way to arrest him, but they were afraid of the crowd because the people held that he was a prophet" (Matthew 21:45-46).

False Praise and Pseudopiety (Matthew 22)

In Matthew 22, the plot thickens. The Pharisees attempted to use deceptive language and false praise to trap Jesus into committing a crime against the Roman state. Matthew 22:15 explicitly states, "Then the Pharisees went out and laid plans to trap him in his words." They began with these odious words of fraudulent admiration:

> They sent their disciples to him along with the Herodians. "Teacher," they said, "we know you are a man of integrity and that you teach the way of God in accordance with the truth. You aren't swayed by men, because you pay no attention to who they are. Tell us then, what is your opinion? Is it right to pay taxes to Caesar or not?" (Matthew 22:16-17)

Jesus was not fooled by their false tribute. He finally had his fill of their legalistic and hypocritical ways, and he answered them,

"You hypocrites, why are you trying to trap me? Show me the coin used for paying the tax." They brought him a denarius, and he asked them, "Whose portrait is this? And whose inscription?" "Caesar's," they replied. Then he said to them, "Give to Caesar what is Caesar's, and to God what is God's." When they heard this, they were amazed. So they left him and went away. (Matthew 22:18-22)

He refused to fall into their ambush. In quick fashion, the Pharisees asked Jesus two more questions. It is obvious that they had been planning the attack for a while because each time he answered their charges to the satisfaction of the crowd, they returned with another challenge.

They asked him to whom we would be married in heaven, especially those who had been married multiple times (Matthew 22:23-32). He responded that there will be no need for sexual intimacy or marriage in heaven, and further responded that they were asking the question because they were ignorant of the Scriptures. Matthew 22:33 records that "when the crowds heard this, they were astonished at his teaching."

Then the Pharisees "tested" Jesus by asking him to identify the greatest commandment. Jesus answered by summarizing the intent of the Law: " 'Love the Lord your God with all your heart and with all your soul and with all your mind.' This is the first and greatest commandment. And the second is like it: 'Love your neighbor as yourself.' All the Law and the Prophets hang on these two commandments" (Matthew 22:37-40).

In each case, however, the Pharisees couched their challenges in fake praise! At the beginning of each disputation, they used the title "Teacher" (Matthew 22:16, 24, 36). The Greek word there is *didaskalos*. It was a word used for one who was worthy of teaching. Certainly, the religious leaders did not *believe* that this man from Nazareth was worthy of teaching the people.

Their "praise" was dripping with sarcasm.

This method of false praise is a form of entrapment. It is deception in its purest (or impurest) form. Legalists who are worried about decorum often pretend to be telling the "truth in love," as Ephesians 4:15 demands, but the "love" is merely manufactured. The only thing they love is the sound of their own voices.

There is nothing worse than false praise as a façade for contempt. These are not my words of wisdom; they are the words of our Lord. Finally, Jesus responded to their constant barrage and attacks, and when he did, it was nothing less than spectacular. It was also a portentous warning to the hypocrite.

Servants, Not Superstars (Matthew 23:1-12)

Jesus responded to the Pharisees, but he did so by speaking first to the crowds: "The teachers of the law and the Pharisees sit in Moses' seat. So you must obey them and do everything they tell you. But do not do what they do, for they do not practice what they preach" (Matthew 23:1-3). He described their hearts' intentions rather than their outward actions, and the indictment was quite startling. Listen to this description, and see if you recognize any symptoms in people you may know:

1. They demand a heavy burden on others, but they themselves will not lift a finger (23:4).
2. Everything they do, they do for show, to earn the adoration of the people (23:5).
3. They love places of honor in the synagogues because they love power (23:6).
4. They love the titles they think they earned and use the title "Rabbi" as an excuse to be considered greater than the people (23:7).
5. They are not servants, but they consider themselves masters (23:8).

The model for ministry set by our Lord is thus one of service. He told the people that being a "servant" is the greatest virtue of a leader. He concluded, "The greatest among you will be your servant. For whoever exalts himself will be humbled, and whoever humbles himself will be exalted" (Matthew 23:11-12). In the world of the pharisee, this is unthinkable.

They make demands on you that they themselves would never follow. They pull the "elder card" when they want to tell you what to do, even though they live by a different standard. They act with false humility, but secretly crave the power for which they have fought. They demand your obedience, even when they are furtively rebellious.

It is a sad admission that churches are filled with these types of incongruent believers. Tragically, they are often in leadership because they are very accomplished at the politics of piety. They turn fellowships that should be filled with joy into power plays and arenas of battle. They ruin our testimony before an unbelieving world.

Beware of the Unteachable Teachers

While I was a pastor in Colorado, there was a young man who transformed right before my eyes. When I first went there, he was filled with an exuberant faith and volunteered to help in countless ways. He rejoiced when people were saved in the church. He helped with the youth group as we sought to change it from an introspective country club to a place open to visitors. He was a joy to be around.

Yet over the course of time, he changed. He began to attend seminary classes, and as we all know, there is nothing more dangerous than a first-year Bible college student! He began to look down on the new believers in the faith. Doctrinally, he became ensnared in a movement that rejected evangelism, instead replacing it with self-centered pursuits of knowledge. It was horrific to watch.

What made it more frustrating was that, as he continued his studies, he slowly stopped attending church. He felt our services were too boisterous and shallow, and our members too excitable. He acted superior to those around him.

The finality of our relationship came when he actually asked to teach a class in the church. Never attending the church, he now wanted to be a leader! He said that he could not find a class where he was "fed" spiritually.

Beware. Underline that word if you must, but *beware of the unteachable teacher*. Pharisees are comfortable only when they are in leadership. They follow no one. They consider themselves better than other believers and develop a haughty spirit that is infectious. Sadly, even the family of this young man was affected by this change. His father, who had faithfully taught a Bible study class for years, changed. He taught his class and then left the church! I assure you, I stopped that quickly.

The Wheel of Woe (Matthew 23:13-33)

When Jesus finally confronted the religious leaders, he spared no condemnation. Seven times in the next twenty verses, he addressed them by stating, "Woe to you . . ." The word *woe* is an exclamation, specifically for expressing grief. We use terms such as *oh my* and *yikes* as exclamations in our modern language. This word (Greek: *ouai*) would roughly be the same as saying, "Horrors!" The Good News Bible translates it into "How terrible for you."

Seven times Jesus expressed his outrage at their false forms of religion. In each case the indictment was followed by a specific spiritual crime they committed in their so-called service to God. The following chart shows the progression of his condemnation:

Matthew	"Woe to you . . ."	Indictment
23:13	Teachers of the law and Pharisees, you hypocrites!	You shut up heaven and do not allow others in!
23:15	Teachers of the law and Pharisees, you hypocrites!	You turn your converts into your own image— sons of hell!
23:16-22	Blind guides!	You make vows by swearing unto the God you rebel against.
23:23-24	Teachers of the law and Pharisees, you hypocrites!	You tithe outwardly but neglect mercy and faith in your hearts!
23:25-26	Teachers of the law and Pharisees, you hypocrites!	You try to clean the outside, but inside you are filthy and sinful.
23:27-28	Teachers of the law and Pharisees, you hypocrites!	You are whitewashed tombs of dead faith.
23:29-30	Teachers of the law and Pharisees, you hypocrites!	You honor the dead but ignore their legacy and teaching. You are guilty!

Quite a set of charges, don't you think? In each condemnation, their sin became increasingly worse. By the time he finished, Jesus compared them to empty tombs, dirty cups, and dead men's bones. They were walking corpses and guilty before God.

When Children of Hell Run the Church

If you want to see how dangerous this type of religion is, notice Jesus' words in Matthew 23:15: "You travel over land and sea to win a single convert, and when he becomes one, you make him twice as much a son of hell as you are." If this type of false faith is allowed to continue, it will become progressively worse.

Each subsequent generation of Pharisees, according to Jesus, was twice as bad as the last. And his condemnation was not a vague notion. He called them "sons of hell." The phrase *huios geenna* could mean one of two things, neither of which is desirable. Either Jesus meant that each generation was twice as deserving of hell as the last, or he meant that they were twice as evil as the last. In either case, it was a strong accusation from our Lord. They were not serving God as they claimed. They were serving the devil.

Could this mean that in our churches and fellowships we have people who are actually working against God? Of course it does. Jesus called them "serpents" and the "brood of vipers" (Matthew 23:33 NKJV). Their venom spreads whenever a church splits and fights. Their actions overwhelm a church and consume its time. They become the center of attention by the sheer weight of their actions.

A pastor friend came under attack by such a group. Though he led a church with thousands in attendance, a small group of about fifty became intent upon firing him. Over the course of a few years, they were consumed with finding charges worthy of firing him. Every single business meeting became a battle. Though it was a megachurch in our modern parlance, it also became a megafight.

They sent out anonymous letters to the membership of the church. They started an anonymous website against him, constantly monitoring his sermons and actions. They posted anonymous blogs. They attacked him on every front, including savage attacks against his integrity and his family.

Eventually, the fight spilled out into the secular world. Because the church was so large, the newspapers and television stations began to report on the squabble that developed into a full-scale war. All over the state, people read about this daily battle.

Intent on his destruction, the group spread their message across our denomination. Leaders received e-mails, faxes, and affidavits of their charges. They took their charges to the courts but were rebuffed every time. He had committed no crime except to stand against them. Yet the small group of disgruntled members would not leave.

Looking back on the fight, one would assume that rapid action could have squashed this battle. After all, what is a group of fifty people against thousands of attending members? The answer lies in the influence of pharisees. Using religious language, such as "we have prayed about this," often makes pharisees feel as if they are on the right side of an argument. It is merely a smokescreen. Pharisees attack anyone in their path, even those who rise and defend their target.

Although thousands attended that church, very few rose to defend the pastor or the church. Tragically, many stopped attending church altogether. Others sat silently and prayed that the fight would go away. Please remember this simple formula for church leadership. Every church is filled with three types of members: Sheep, Goats, and Wolves. A true leader has three responsibilities: Love the Sheep, Convert the Goats, Kill the Wolves.

Because the members of that church did not act to stop the small band of the "sons of hell," they let the wolves win. The pastor eventually resigned from the church.

> *Every church is filled with three types of members: Sheep, Goats, and Wolves. A true leader has three responsibilities: Love the Sheep, Convert the Goats, Kill the Wolves.*

Broken Hearts and Bruised Faith (Matthew 23:37-39)

What is the consequence of inaction? What happens if we ignore the legalist and the libertine? Do they go away? Does the problem eventually just fade into the background? Of course not. You must take action.

After Jesus confronted the Pharisees, he lamented over Jerusalem. His voice cracked with grief as he cried out: "O

Jerusalem, Jerusalem, the one who kills the prophets and stones those who are sent to her! How often I wanted to gather your children together, as a hen gathers her chicks under her wings, but you were not willing!" (Matthew 23:37 NKJV).

It broke the heart of the Lord that such a small band of poisonous men could turn the hearts of the people against him. Remember, seven days before his crucifixion, Jesus was greeted by throngs of people shouting, "Hosanna!" At the end, the same crowd called for his death.

Did the people suddenly change their opinions?

No.

The infection of the Pharisees was enough to get people to go along.

Maintaining the freedom and joy of your faith in Jesus is not going to happen by accident. You must search diligently for it. You must be vigilant against the poison of those who are toxins to your spiritual life.

You may be bruised, but you are not beaten. Joyous faith is worth fighting for.

Resurrection and Rebirth (Matthew 27–28)

Do toxic Christians ever recover and reclaim the joy of their salvation? The question may be obvious, but the answer is more complex. Even though Christians become toxic for many reasons, there is only one cure for the poison that saps their souls. For there to be healing, they must again become open to experience the love and grace of Jesus Christ in a deeper and richer way.

God heals in many ways. We may wish for toxic Christians to be struck with an instantaneous bolt of love. But God also heals through medical science, and depression can trigger toxic faith, as can unresolved trauma. But for some, only death will bring the final healing.

When the disciples gave up all hope, they met the risen Savior, who gave them a mission: to go into the world and make disciples. In other words, we are saved to live with joy and to serve and love others. We are called to serve by being in mission to the least, the last, and the lost—binding their wounds by offering solace and maybe Meals on Wheels. We are called to love friends and enemies, meeting their needs and working for God's justice. Yet no one works alone. The Gospel of Matthew ends with Jesus' promise to be with us forever. We serve a risen Savior who graciously walks beside us, always teaching, guiding, and loving so that we can live with a vibrant faith.

CHAPTER TEN

Detox: A Formula for Authentic Faith

Now there was a man of the Pharisees named Nicodemus, a
member of the Jewish ruling council. He came to Jesus at night
and said, "Rabbi, we know you are a teacher who has come from
God. For no one could perform the miraculous signs you are
doing if God were not with him." In reply Jesus declared, "I tell
you the truth, no one can see the kingdom of God unless he is
born again." "How can a man be born when he is old?"
Nicodemus asked. "Surely he cannot enter a second time into his
mother's womb to be born!" Jesus answered, "I tell you the
truth, no one can enter the kingdom of God unless he is born of
water and the Spirit. Flesh gives birth to flesh, but the Spirit
gives birth to spirit. You should not be surprised at my saying,
'You must be born again.' The wind blows wherever it pleases.
You hear its sound, but you cannot tell where it comes from or
where it is going. So it is with everyone born of the Spirit."
"How can this be?" Nicodemus asked. "You are Israel's
teacher," said Jesus, "and do you not understand these things? I
tell you the truth, we speak of what we know, and we testify to
what we have seen, but still you people do not accept our testi-
mony. I have spoken to you of earthly things and you do not
believe; how then will you believe if I speak of heavenly things?
No one has ever gone into heaven except the one who came from
heaven—the Son of Man." (John 3:1-13)

You Can Go Home Again

In the spring of 2008, I had the opportunity to return to the
church where I came to faith in Jesus Christ. Stelzer Road Baptist
Church was sold about a decade ago because its membership had
dwindled to only a handful. The pastor who had led me to Christ

had retired, and subsequent pastors had not grown the fellowship. Eventually, the decision was made to sell the facility to a sister church that needed a building. The sign was taken down and the rooms were emptied. The money from the sale went to the association, and other church starts benefited from the funds.

Stelzer Road Church was no more.

The building looks remarkably the same, however. The brick U-shaped one-story building still stands, surrounded by trees and forest. The old basketball hoop, now crooked, is in the backyard where we used to play twenty-five years ago. The gravel parking lot still creaks under the weight of approaching cars. The name has changed, but the building remains intact.

It was a bittersweet return. A quarter of a century had passed since I walked those hallways. In many ways, that building was my "rock of remembrance." I was saved and baptized there. I preached my first sermon there. I was ordained there. It was my spiritual delivery room. It was a Saturday afternoon and the building was empty. There were no cars in the lot. The silence was deafening.

As I stood there, I was overwhelmed by emotion. I longed to hear the pastor's voice once again, beckoning us at the Bible study hour. I wished I could hear the piano play one more time. I wanted to hear the sound of voices raised to God just once more.

It was here that I found a new family after I was disowned. It was here that I found acceptance in Christ when I was rejected by my own. I was more than melancholy; I was devastated. I realize that rites of passage are necessary, but the flood of regret and remorse seemed too much to handle.

Suddenly, I heard the sound of my son Drake. I had taken my four-year-old on the trip, and he was oblivious to my stumbling down memory lane. He was happily running around in the front yard of the church, pretending to be a car.

"Papa, look at me!" he exclaimed. He was showing me how his race car was faster than all the others. I smiled at his innocence but remained immobile. I was having one of those lifetime moments when the past collides with the present.

Suddenly, Drake stopped playing as his short attention was diverted.

"Look, Papa!" he yelled once again, this time pointing upward.

"Dat's the cross!" he said in his four-year-old tongue. "Dat's where Jesus lives!"

In one sentence, Drake preached a sermon to me. The building was unimportant. The occupant was. Shaken from my haze of self-pity, I sheepishly looked at my son and said, "Yes, son. Jesus lives here too."

It Is Never Too Late to Detoxify

If this book were to end with the verbal combat between the Lord and the Pharisees throughout the Gospel of Matthew, one might be tempted to despair for our friends who are similarly poisonous. It seems as if the religious leaders of Jesus' day never did learn the lessons that he was so patiently trying to teach them. They succeeded, albeit temporarily, in silencing Jesus and bringing about his crucifixion. They made the charges stick before Pilate, even though Pilate never quite agreed with their interpretation of the law. He never quite went along with their plan, though he did little to stop them.

Even after the resurrection and ascension of our Lord, the religious leaders continued to hound the disciples. Acts 23 records Paul's confrontation with the Sanhedrin, which broke out in violence:

> Paul looked straight at the Sanhedrin and said, "My brothers, I have fulfilled my duty to God in all good conscience to this day." At this the high priest Ananias ordered those standing near Paul to strike him on the mouth. Then Paul said to him, "God will strike you, you whitewashed wall! You sit there to judge me according to the law, yet you yourself violate the law by commanding that I be struck!" (vv. 1-3)

To make matters even worse, when some of the religious leaders did convert and accept Jesus Christ as Lord, they still caused dissension in the churches! Acts 15:5 records that "some of the believers who belonged to the party of the Pharisees stood up and said, 'The Gentiles must be circumcised and required to obey the law of Moses.' "

They were consistent—making demands on believers whom Jesus did not teach. Where Jesus brought liberty through grace, these believers were still demanding that legalistic rules be followed. Perhaps they were too soon removed from their past lives as Pharisees, but they certainly stirred up trouble within the fellowship.

If this were the end of the tale, we would be left with the feeling that there was no hope for these people. As you have gone through this study, you may have been mentally writing the names of people in the margins. If the last chapter were the final adjudication, these friends would be cast off as hopeless cases of legalistic bondage.

But the Bible records a successful rehabilitation story.

According to the Bible, Nicodemus triumphantly completed detox.

Nicodemus the Notorious Inquisitor (John 3:1-13)

Few characters in Scripture are as famous as Nicodemus. Because of the clarity of Jesus' words in the chapter, children are taught this story from the time they are in the nursery. The most famous verse in the chapter is John 3:16, which is one of the first verses that new believers memorize. For God so loved the world . . .

Yet we usually rush past the context of the chapter. Nicodemus was called a Pharisee and a member of the Jewish ruling council. He was obviously a man of great influence and intense training. He was also probably well known in Jerusalem because when he decided to approach Jesus, he did it under the stealth of night. If he had been seen speaking to Jesus in the daytime, perhaps he would have been ridiculed or even been considered a collaborator.

We usually scoff at Nicodemus's misunderstanding of Jesus' teachings. In the most elementary fashion, Nicodemus seemed to recoil at the simple clarity of our Savior's words, "You must be born again."

John 3:4 records Nicodemus asking, "How can a man be born when he is old?" After Jesus explained the new birth to him, he again asked, "How can this be?" (John 3:9). On the surface, it seems that Nicodemus's heart is too calloused and too impertinent to understand the essentials of the faith.

Not so fast.

Read the rest of the book. *Nicodemus was changed by this meeting.*

Nicodemus the Public Defender (John 7:47-53)

An angry mob of religious rulers confronted Jesus during the Feast of Tabernacles (John 7). Jesus offered Living Water to those who were thirsty and explicitly made the claim to his divinity. In cruel scorn, the Pharisees rejected his claim and even attempted to show that they were unanimous in their belief that he should be put to death.

Yet one man spoke up. One Pharisee attempted to defend Jesus in a most unusual manner. John 7:45-53 records the dramatic scene:

> Finally the temple guards went back to the chief priests and Pharisees, who asked them, "Why didn't you bring him in?" "No one ever spoke the way this man does," the guards declared. "You mean he has deceived you also?" the Pharisees retorted. "Has any of the rulers or of the Pharisees believed in him? No! But this mob that knows nothing of the law—there is a curse on them." *Nicodemus, who had gone to Jesus earlier and who was one of their own number, asked,* "Does our law condemn anyone without first hearing him to find out what he is doing?" They replied, "Are you from Galilee, too? Look into it, and you will find that a prophet does not come out of Galilee." Then each went to his own home. (emphasis added)

This is the first recorded instance of a disagreement among the Pharisees themselves! Certainly, the Pharisees had disputed with the other groups, such as the Sadducees, but now one of their own spoke up for Jesus. Nicodemus asked that Jesus be heard before a sentence was handed down arbitrarily.

This action was so remarkable that John gave the disclaimer, "Nicodemus, who had gone to Jesus earlier and who was one of their own number . . ." Imagine—Nicodemus had progressed from speaking to Jesus secretly at night to speaking boldly before his own brethren. The bravery of the action is reflected in the response of the other Pharisees. They offered Nicodemus a mild rebuke, and then they went to their homes.

In one swift statement Nicodemus had defused a potentially threatening situation.

Nicodemus the Pallbearer (John 19:38-42)

Perhaps the most remarkable transition in the life of Nicodemus took place after the crucifixion of our Lord. Although all of the disciples except John had gone into hiding, two men remained: Joseph of Arimathea and Nicodemus. In John 19, we read:

> Later, Joseph of Arimathea asked Pilate for the body of Jesus. Now Joseph was a disciple of Jesus, but secretly because he feared the Jews. With Pilate's permission, he came and took the body away. *He was accompanied by Nicodemus, the man who earlier had visited Jesus at night. Nicodemus brought a mixture of myrrh and aloes, about seventy-five pounds.* Taking Jesus' body, the two of them wrapped it, with the spices, in strips of linen. This was in accordance with Jewish burial customs. At the place where Jesus was crucified, there was a garden, and in the garden a new tomb, in which no one had ever been laid. Because it was the Jewish day of Preparation and since the tomb was nearby, they laid Jesus there. (vv. 38-42, emphasis added)

The gallantry of their act cannot be overstated. Both men had secretly been followers of Christ, and yet they were publicly treating the body of the condemned criminal with the same care that would be extended to a faithful Jew! Like the soldiers planting the flag at Iwo Jima, these two men defiantly cared for his body. Biblical scholars are almost unanimous in their conclusion that Nicodemus was not only a believer in Christ by this point, but he was publicly emphatic in his faith.

The Healing of the Pharisee Nicodemus

How could a man so entrenched in legalism, tradition, and toxic religion become such a vocal and vibrant believer? The same question can be asked of our friends and family. The road to spiritual healing is not impossible, but neither is it easy. Toxic faith does not have to be lethal.

First, Nicodemus began to find healing when he took his questions directly to Jesus. In the third chapter of John, we read of this interview but often miss the first point: Nicodemus came to Jesus.

He did not seek the opinions of others.

He did not rest on traditions alone.

He did not simply believe rumors.

He went directly to Jesus with his concerns.

The first step to detoxification is retracing your first steps as a new believer. Do you remember when you held the word of God in your hands with a sense of awe? Do you remember when you first opened a biblical text and were *excited* to discover the truths therein? If we believe there is power in the word of God, we must be willing to go *first* to the Bible, before all other books.

This is a monumentally difficult assignment. We are surrounded by well-written commentaries, lucid biblical study, and detailed philosophies. It is tempting to go *first* to the commentaries, to get someone else's interpretation of the text. However, have you ever asked yourself, *Why do I go to the commentaries first?*

Commentaries and the writings of men and women are wonderful supplements to the Bible. But please remember—they are supplements. Could you imagine trying to live by eating only vitamins? Minerals and vitamins are a wonderful complement to a healthy diet, but they are not replacements for a healthy diet.

When we become aware of the descent into toxic living, we are often vulnerable to these poisons because we have not received the proper nourishment of the Word. We begin to fight over traditions and doctrinal divisions that may seem at first to be inconsequential. We begin to take sides. When our philosophies dictate our theology, this is a sure sign of poisonous faith. Getting back into the undiluted and unfiltered study of the Bible is a refreshing means of healing. Like Nicodemus, we bring our doubts and questions to the one who can answer us directly.

Second, Nicodemus was willing to ask difficult questions. There was very little pomp in his direct questions. He had little time for decorum. Nicodemus was a man on a mission, and he did not couch his questions in deceit. Often Christians intentionally avoid the difficult questions because they make us uncomfortable. Eventually, the actual question is lost in a flood of words. We forego the search for answers because others may think our faith is weak.

We surrender to silence.

Yet the strongest faith is a tested faith. I often tell my students that I live by one prevailing axiom: an unexamined life is not worth

> *An unexamined life is not worth living, and an unexamined faith is not worth holding.*

living, and an unexamined faith is not worth holding.

By building off the classic Greek philosophical statement, I bring faith into the mix. If I regularly live by a blind and untested faith, then the first time someone challenges my assumptions, my entire belief system falls.

This explains why so many students lose their faith once they get to college. They have been told since childhood that we believe these core truths, but they are never invited to ask *why* we believe these truths. When a professor rises to challenge their worldview, it cannot withstand the attack, and their faith crumbles.

Nicodemus was not willing to settle for a cursory understanding of Jesus' teachings—he wanted to know *why*. It was an admirable trait that obviously bore fruit in his life.

Finally, he was willing to lay aside his preconceived notions about faith and truth. As a Pharisee, Nicodemus had extensive training in Jewish law and tradition. He had diligently studied the texts and teachings of his forefathers. Yet he was willing to be open-minded. That was a key component to Nicodemus's rehabilitation. He was willing to listen.

Often we become toxic when we become intractable. Entrenched in our own systems, we no longer seek truth. Many believers become poisoned when they become unteachable. They believe they have attained all truth and knowledge, and they no longer hunger and thirst after righteousness.

My Rehabilitation and Detox

In the end, this was the path to my healing and liberation. I was able to release my anger when I became like a new believer again. I was shocked to read that the church at Ephesus was doctrinally sound but spiritually weak. God warned them that they had lost their "first love" (Revelation 2:4).

I had become a charter member of the church at Ephesus.

My joy had been replaced by duty.

My compassion had been replaced by judgment.

My hunger had been replaced by a false sense of satiation.

My sin was pride.

There is a tremendous difference between following the ministry as a vocation and following it as a calling. I can be trained to give the right answers, but only God can give me discernment. I can study to get knowledge, but only God can give me wisdom. I am not called to be a professional Christian; I am called to be a faithful Christian.

The profundity of the last paragraph is a summary of a journey of a number of years in my life. It does not record the number of sleepless nights I spent, wondering if I misunderstood God's call. It does not detail the numbness in my heart when I attempted to muster fake tears in the face of someone else's grief. All I can tell you, dear reader, is that I reached a point in my spiritual journey where I wanted to quit. I could not interpret my emotions at the time. Perhaps I felt that I had let God down. Perhaps I felt that God had let me down.

In the end, I discovered that I had fallen into a subtle trap of robotic, unfeeling, and unintentional pharisaical ministry. I was promised eternal life but was miserable here on earth. It took the community of faith—the testimonies of countless vibrant Christians—to cut through the layers of spiritual calluses I had developed. It took the resplendent joy of a four-year-old boy to renew my passion for serving Christ again. It took receiving a deeper, richer love of God to saturate my soul.

I pray your journey ends well, regardless where you are today.

Teaching Questions and Themes

Chapter	Matthew	Chapter Title	Question	Diagnosis and Theme
1	5:17-20	For There to Be Winners, There Also Have to Be Losers	Who is great in the kingdom of heaven?	Toxic Christians never ask questions because they know all the answers.
2	9:9-13	The Holy Huddle	Who is righteous, and who is a sinner?	Toxic Christians avoid contact with the lost.
3	9:14-17	The Great Pretenders	Why do you not fast?	Toxic Christians are obsessed with comparison.
4	12:1-13	How Dare You Help?	Why do you do unlawful things on the Sabbath?	Toxic Christians embrace obedience over mercy.
5	12:38-45	Signs, Signs, Everywhere Are Signs	Why don't you show us a sign?	Toxic Christians are suspicious people.
6	15:1-14	The Dead Faith of the Living	Why do you break with tradition?	Toxic Christians equate preference with principle.
7	16:1-12	Church of the Frozen Smile	How is it that you still don't understand?	Toxic Christians suffer from inauthentic faith.
8	19:1-12	Anyone Got Some Rocks?	What are the limits of the Law?	Toxic Christians follow the letter of the Law, but not the Spirit.
9	22–28	When Jesus Lays the Smack Down	Why do you shut heaven's door on others? Why be born again?	You must respond to toxic faith—it will not simply go away. New life means a deeper faith.